BEYOND LOVING THE ENVIRONMENT

SECOND EDITION

FROM CLIMATE SCIENCE TO CARBON GOVERNANCE, CIRCULAR ECONOMY AND ESG TRANSFORMATION

DR. SRI UMESWARAN SHEKAR

notionpress.com

INDIA · SINGAPORE · MALAYSIA

ISBN 979-8-90342-680-5

Dedication

To future generations. May you inherit a planet that is cleaner, greener, and wiser than the one we received.

CONTENTS

FOREWORD

Dato' Dr. Nadzri Bin Yahaya
Former Deputy Secretary-General,
Ministry of Natural Resources and Environmental Sustainability
(NRES) Malaysia

This second publication by Dr. Sri Umeswaran, titled *'Beyond Loving the Environment'*, reflects the complexity of efforts to ensure environmental protection and conservation. Yesterday's issues will fester into today's problems if not solved holistically, and new and emerging issues will continue to hinder our efforts to sustain a safe, healthy, and progressive environment if they are not addressed in our sustainability agenda.

A comprehensive approach is essential, one that combines policy and strategies, legislative instruments, and incorporates innovative approaches and out-of-the-box thinking. Most importantly, however, the responsibility for keeping sustainable development on track rests on changing the mindset of the population, which includes both the community and industry players. Thus, it is enlightening that the book addresses several pertinent subjects such as the circular economy which is a popular topic of discussion aimed at ensuring waste is "not wasted" but becomes a resource and ESG, which helps align our governance to be more structured, transparent, and focused. Last but not least, the book also looks into the importance of industry players maintaining production in tandem with their responsibility for a clean environment.

"Think global and act local" is a popular slogan that maintains a bridge between national and international efforts to keep this planet green and productive. Although domestic efforts may seem small, they will surely and confidently contribute to the successful implementation of multilateral environmental agreements, such as those on climate change and ozone-depleting substances. Thus, it is heartening that the book also includes a perspective on international environmental governance.

In conclusion, this edition of *'Beyond Loving the Environment'* is a valuable reference and guide for those who work passionately toward ensuring sustainable development and loving the environment.

FOREWORD

Mr. Raja Singham
Managing Director & Chief Future Officer
Brickfields Asia College (BAC) Education Group

"The defining challenge of the 21st century is not whether we care about the Earth, it is whether we can redesign our systems in time to protect it."

For much of modern history, environmental stewardship was framed as a moral responsibility, a call for individuals and societies to care for the natural world. Today, the scale and urgency of environmental change have fundamentally altered that conversation.

Climate instability, biodiversity loss, resource depletion, and ecological disruption are no longer distant concerns debated only in scientific circles. They are realities shaping economies, influencing global trade, and redefining the responsibilities of governments, corporations, and citizens alike.

Sustainability is no longer merely an environmental issue. It is an economic, legal, and governance imperative.

In '*Beyond Loving the Environment*', Dr. Sri Umeswaran takes us beyond awareness and into the architecture of solutions. This book shows that environmental protection cannot rely on good intentions alone. It requires systemic transformation aligning law, policy, finance, technology, and societal behaviour toward a sustainable future.

What distinguishes this work is its integrated perspective. Rather than treating climate change, circular economy principles, ESG governance, and sustainable finance as separate domains, the author demonstrates how these forces interact to reshape modern economies.

Environmental risk is increasingly financial risk and financial risk ultimately becomes systemic risk.

When environmental stability is threatened, economic stability inevitably follows.

This book provides an important framework for understanding that reality. It bridges academic insight with practical governance, offering perspectives for policymakers, corporate leaders, financial institutions, and citizens seeking to navigate a rapidly evolving world.

As someone deeply engaged in the future of education, I find particular inspiration in the author's journey. Dr. Sri Umeswaran combines expertise in sustainability governance with legal scholarship as a part-time law student at BAC. His work reflects a belief we hold strongly: education should empower individuals not only to succeed professionally, but also to address the defining challenges of their generation.

The environmental transformation ahead will not be achieved through incremental change. It will require coordinated leadership across governments, markets, institutions, and communities.

The sustainability transition is not simply about protecting nature. It is about safeguarding the long-term resilience of human civilisation.

Books such as '*Beyond Loving the Environment*' help move the conversation beyond rhetoric toward strategy and beyond awareness toward action.

The future will belong to those who do more than recognise the crisis. It will belong to those with the courage to redesign the systems that created it.

FOREWORD

Dr. Margaret Kuyor
Deputy Undersecretary (Circular Economy Policy)
Urban Sustainability Division
Ministry of Housing and Local Government, Malaysia

Sustainability today is no longer just an environmental issue. It has become part of a broader effort to rethink how we manage resources, design policies, and build systems that balance economic growth with environmental protection. Governments, industries, and communities all play an important role in this transition. In this context, *Beyond Loving the Environment* by Dr. Sri Umeswaran provides a timely reflection on the challenges and opportunities ahead.

Over the years, working with Dr. Sri Umeswaran, he has actively contributed to discussions on solid waste management and the circular economy in Malaysia. As a friend of the industry, he is often remembered for his insights into the role of the informal sector in recycling systems. At the same time, his contributions extend beyond this area, including work related to the Circular Economy Blueprint for Solid Waste, Extended Producer Responsibility (EPR), Pay-As-You-Throw mechanisms, and broader discussions on sustainable waste management practices.

I sincerely appreciate his long-standing contributions and insights in advancing solid waste management in Malaysia. Even when we may approach certain issues from different angles, I believe our shared intention remains the same, to strengthen Malaysia's waste management system and move the country forward toward a circular economy and a more sustainable nation for our future generations.

FOREWORD

Dr. Jayaprakash Murulitharan
PhD in Chemistry (Atmospheric Science)
University of Cambridge

History rarely announces structural change politely. It reveals itself through crisis, instability, and the gradual realisation that existing systems are no longer sufficient to sustain prosperity, equity, or peace.

We are living in such a moment.

Climate volatility, biodiversity loss, supply chain fragility, capital market recalibration, and social inequality are not isolated disruptions. They are signals that the economic model of the past century has reached its structural limits. Sustainability, therefore, is not a matter of environmental preference. It is the organising principle of the next era of economic development.

In *Beyond Loving the Environment*, Dr. Sri Umeswaran advances a proposition that is both urgent and profound: the transition before us is not sectoral reform but systemic redesign. The book does not treat sustainability as a peripheral obligation of industry or a moral extension of environmentalism. Instead, it frames sustainability as the foundational architecture for resilient economies, credible institutions, and stable societies.

The integrated framework outlined in this book, covering governance and policy architecture, sustainable finance and capital allocation, technological innovation and industrial transition, as well as behavioural and cultural change, acknowledges that transformation cannot happen in isolated parts. Regulation without capital alignment will fail. Innovation lacking governance discipline will distort outcomes. Finance without ethical accountability will cause instability. Behavioural change without structural incentives will remain superficial.

True transition requires coherence.

This work is distinguished by its insistence on implementation. It confronts the realities of circular economy deployment, Extended Producer Responsibility enforcement, ESG regulatory transformation, climate-finance evolution, and international environmental governance not as theoretical aspirations but as institutional imperatives. It bridges scholarship and statecraft, corporate governance and public policy, financial markets and legislative coordination.

In doing so, it positions Malaysia within a broader regional and global recalibration, not as a passive participant but as a jurisdiction capable of shaping credible sustainability architecture within ASEAN and beyond. The emphasis on policy integration and governance reform recognises a truth increasingly acknowledged across continents: environmental stability and economic resilience are inseparable conditions of national security and long-term competitiveness.

The transition ahead is unavoidable. Markets are readjusting. Capital is reassessing risk. Citizens are demanding transparency. Younger generations are redefining what matters. Institutions that fail to adapt will not just underperform; they will become fundamentally obsolete.

Yet within this challenge lies a historic opportunity.

Nations that design coherent sustainability frameworks will attract capital, talent, and innovation. Corporations that embed ESG accountability into strategic governance will command trust. Financial institutions that integrate climate risk into allocation decisions will shape the contours of future growth. Societies that cultivate responsible consumption will strengthen social cohesion and intergenerational equity.

This book offers a structured roadmap for such transformation. It serves as a university reference, a policy handbook, a corporate governance guide, and a sustainability framework precisely because the transition it describes transcends institutional boundaries. It recognises that the sustainability era will not be led by any single actor. It will be shaped by alignment between the state and the market, innovation and regulation, and growth and stewardship.

Above all, this book affirms a principle that will shape the coming decades: economic systems must now operate within ecological limits rather than against them. Prosperity must be regenerative, not extractive. Growth must be resilient, not fragile.

We stand at a pivotal moment in modern economic history. The real question is not whether change will happen, but whether we will shape it intentionally, with foresight, coherence, and institutional bravery, or let it be forced upon us through crisis.

Dr. Sri Umeswaran's work contributes meaningfully to the deliberate path. This volume marks Dr. Sri Umeswaran's second publication, building upon the foundation established by his first book, *Love the Environment* (2015), and advancing its central themes into a more comprehensive and systemic sustainability framework.

It is with conviction that I commend *Beyond Loving the Environment* to policymakers, regulators, financial leaders, scholars, and citizens committed to designing a future in which sustainability is not a slogan, but a structural foundation of enduring prosperity.

FOREWORD

Professor Dr. Yuka Fujimoto
Professor of Business Management & Deputy Dean
(Research & Sustainability)
Sunway Business School, Sunway University, Malaysia

Sustainability is no longer a peripheral environmental concern, it requires a structural economic transformation that protects and sustains our planet. The book calls for redefining how nations design policy, how markets allocate capital, how corporations take responsibility for the natural environment, and how societies coordinate collective action. This Second Edition presents sustainability not as incremental reform, but as systemic transformation across every sector anchored in the realities of Malaysia's evolving economic and institutional landscape.

What distinguishes this volume is its integrative insight. Rather than treating sustainability as a fragmented agenda dispersed across environmental policy, corporate social responsibility, or technological innovation, the book coherently reflects the structural interdependencies among different actors and sectors required to address societal grand challenges in a coordinated and economically viable manner. The strength of this work lies in its ability to bridge domains that are often examined in isolation. It advances theory (i.e., new conceptual insights) by encouraging every actor to see the bigger picture and understand how he or she can play a role within an integrated ecosystem rather than through standalone initiatives. Importantly, it recognizes that sustainability transitions require not only institutional reform but also shifts in organizational behaviour, capital allocation logic, and consumption patterns.

For Malaysia, this framing is particularly timely and important. As the country navigates industrial transition, green technology development, and regional competitiveness within ASEAN and global markets, sustainability becomes inseparable from economic resilience. The book situates Malaysia within broader international developments while offering a grounded roadmap for governments, regulators, corporations, financial institutions, academia, and civil society. It may serve as a university reference text, a policy handbook, a corporate ESG guide, and a sustainability governance framework. Such versatility reflects the structural nature of the transition it describes.

The central message of this book is clear: environmental stability and economic stability are not competing objectives a perspective that I fundamentally agree must form the core DNA of a sustainable future. They are structurally interdependent.

In *Beyond Loving the Environment*, Dr. Sri Umeswaran offers both conceptual clarity and practical direction, providing readers with a rigorous yet accessible framework to understand sustainability as systemic transformation and, more importantly, to act upon it.

FOREWORD

Associate Professor Dr. Mahyuddin Daud
Director, Student Affairs and Development Division
International Islamic University Malaysia Cum Associate Professor of Law,
Ahmad Ibrahim Kulliyyah of Laws, International Islamic
University Malaysia

The global conversation on sustainability has evolved dramatically over the past decade. What was once largely framed as environmental protection is now widely recognised as a fundamental transformation of our economic systems, governance structures, and societal values. In this context, *Beyond Loving the Environment* by Dr. Sri Umeswaran arrives at a particularly important moment. In this new volume, the author extends that conversation significantly by moving beyond awareness to address the structural transformations required to achieve genuine sustainability.

This book positions sustainability not only as a peripheral environmental concern but as a systemic reconfiguration of how economies function and how societies organise production, consumption, and governance. The work recognises that environmental stability, economic resilience, and social responsibility are inseparable elements of a single development paradigm.

One of the strengths of this book lies in its integrated framework built around four interdependent pillars: governance and policy architecture, sustainable finance and capital allocation, technological innovation and industrial transition, and behavioural and cultural transformation. By bringing these dimensions together, Dr. Sri provides a comprehensive perspective on sustainability that reflects the complexity of contemporary environmental and economic challenges.

Particularly noteworthy is the book's exploration of emerging governance and regulatory mechanisms, including Extended Producer Responsibility (EPR), ESG accountability frameworks, and evolving climate finance systems. These instruments are increasingly shaping the way governments regulate industries and how corporations respond to environmental risks and responsibilities. The author's discussion of circular economy models further highlights the need to rethink resource use and production systems in ways that minimise waste while maximising long-term value creation.

The transition towards sustainable economies is no longer optional. It is an inevitable structural shift that will define the resilience and competitiveness of nations in the coming decades. Works such as *Beyond Loving the Environment* play an important role in helping society understand the scale of this transformation and the pathways available to achieve it.

I commend Dr. Sri Umeswaran for producing a thoughtful and timely contribution to the sustainability discourse. It is my hope that this book will inspire policymakers, scholars, practitioners, and citizens alike to engage more deeply with the urgent task of building a sustainable future.

FOREWORD

Dr. Umawathy Techanamurthy
Senior Lecture, Engineering Education Department
Universiti Kebangsaan Malaysia

Sustainability has long been framed as an environmental concern, often confined to discussions about conservation, resource protection, or ecological responsibility. Today, however, it has become clear that sustainability represents something far more profound: a systemic transformation of how societies organise their economies, institutions, and ways of life. Environmental stability is no longer merely an aspiration of environmentalists; it is a structural condition for economic resilience, social wellbeing, and long-term development.

In this timely and ambitious second edition, Dr. Sri Umeswaran moves beyond the foundational ideas presented in his earlier work, *Love the Environment* (2015), to present a more comprehensive and forward-looking examination of sustainability in the contemporary era. *Beyond Loving the Environment* recognises that awareness alone is no longer sufficient. The global sustainability agenda now demands coordinated policy frameworks, institutional accountability, technological innovation, and meaningful behavioural change.

What distinguishes this book is its clear recognition that sustainability cannot be addressed through isolated sectoral initiatives. Rather, it must be understood as a systems transformation. The framework presented here thoughtfully integrates governance, finance, technological transition, and societal behaviour into a coherent structure. This multidimensional approach reflects the complexity of the sustainability challenge and the need for solutions that operate across policy, industry, and civil society.

The book provides an expansive exploration of critical areas shaping the global sustainability discourse today. These include the implementation of the circular economy, the enforcement of Extended Producer Responsibility (EPR), the growing significance of Environmental, Social and Governance (ESG) accountability, the evolution of climate finance, and the role of innovation ecosystems in enabling sustainable industrial transitions. By bringing together these themes, the author demonstrates that sustainability is not merely a technical matter but a governance challenge that requires coordination across multiple domains of decision-making.

Importantly, the work situates Malaysia within the broader regional and international sustainability landscape. As countries across the world accelerate their commitments to climate action, responsible resource management, and green economic transformation, Malaysia too is navigating an important transition. This book provides valuable insight into how regulatory design, corporate governance, and policy coordination can contribute to shaping a more resilient and sustainable national development trajectory.

Another strength of this volume lies in its ability to bridge diverse audiences. Scholars will appreciate the conceptual grounding and structured analysis of sustainability systems. Policymakers will find a thoughtful discussion of regulatory instruments and governance mechanisms. Corporate leaders and financial institutions will recognise the growing importance of ESG integration and sustainable investment strategies. Equally, civil society actors and educators will benefit from the book's emphasis on behavioural change and sustainable lifestyles.

In an era marked by accelerating climate risks, biodiversity loss, and resource pressures, the sustainability transition is no longer optional. It represents a fundamental redesign of economic systems and governance frameworks. Books such as this play an important role in guiding that transition by connecting academic knowledge, policy innovation, and practical implementation.

Dr. Sri Umeswaran's work contributes meaningfully to this dialogue by offering both conceptual clarity and practical direction. *Beyond Loving the Environment* invites readers to think beyond awareness toward structural change, encouraging institutions, industries, and individuals alike to recognise their role in shaping a sustainable future.

It is therefore a privilege to introduce this important contribution. I hope that this book will stimulate thoughtful discussion, inspire responsible leadership, and support the collective efforts needed to build a more sustainable and resilient world.

FOREWORD

Dr. Gary W. Theseira
Council Chairman, Climate Governance Malaysia
Adjunct Associate Professor, Asia School of Business in collaboration with MIT Sloan Management

It gives me great pleasure to, firstly, congratulate Dr. Sri Umeswaran Shekar on the publication of his second book, '*Beyond Loving the Environment*', and secondly, to share some brief thoughts in a foreword.

Environmental advocates have always faced a difficult dilemma. On the one hand, they believe very deeply that a knowledgeable and informed public will better understand what needs to be done to keep human civilization alive and thriving on this planet. But on the other hand, they know full well that humans are more likely to take action when motivated by emotion, rather than by logic or reasoning. So they have had to walk a thin line, trying to educate without sounding condescending, trying to exhort without sounding preachy, and trying to motivate without sounding alarmist.

In his second book, Dr. Sri Umeswaran builds on the comprehensive set of themes addressed in his first book, adopting a systems approach that is at the same time both ambitions and realistic. Ambitious in that it unabashedly champions the view that transitioning to sustainability requires far more than sectoral reform; in fact, it demands a complete and far-reaching systemic redesign. Taking an uncompromising and unapologetic stance on Circularity, Extended Producer Responsibility, and the links to National Legislative Frameworks and Human Consumption Behavior, he zeroes in on the must-haves that necessarily underpin the sustainability transition at global, national, and sub-national levels.

Realistic in that it acknowledges that the myriad parts that comprise the entire ecosystem of human socio-economic activities, all need to be functioning and delivering seamlessly to populate the pipeline of sustainability initiatives, from the technologically nascent, to the economically mature. Realistic too, in realizing that only an intact ecosystem could shift the trajectory of anthropogenic greenhouse gas emissions, very literally, to a level humanity could actually live with, and to return humanity to, once again, living within our generous planetary boundaries. Among others, he highlights the central role of Governance and Policy, the catalytic role of Finance and Capital, the facilitating role of Technology and Industrial Innovation, and, importantly, the need for a systems transformation roadmap, guided by future-casting using both global and national scenarios.

Intended as a reference for all who are actively seeking greater impact in their sustainability-related work, *'Beyond Loving the Environment'*, weaves the independent themes of Dr. Sri Umeswaran's first work into a systems-oriented framework of modules that stakeholders, including both public and corporate policy and decision-makers, policy implementers, regulators, and enforcement, can understand, identify with, and confidently apply in their day-to-day choices and decisions. In doing so he has equipped this generation of sustainability advocates with some of the most effective and practical tools with which to improve societal resilience and restore equity, human dignity and noble and ethical values.

PREFACE

When I first began writing about sustainability, it was still considered a specialised topic.

Today, sustainability defines economic survival.

Environmental disruption is no longer theoretical. It is visible in flood events, heatwaves, supply chain instability, and rising adaptation costs. The question is no longer whether transition will occur but how structured and equitable that transition will be.

This Second Edition expands the original vision into a comprehensive academic policy hybrid framework. It integrates governance, finance, innovation, and behavioural transformation into a unified pathway.

This book is written for policymakers who design frameworks, for regulators who enforce them, for corporations navigating ESG obligations, for academics studying structural reform, and for citizens who understand that sustainability is a shared responsibility.

Sustainability is not a trend. It is a generational obligation. The future will not be shaped by rhetoric, but by alignment between policy, capital, technology and culture.

This work is an invitation to build that alignment.

Dr. Sri Umeswaran Shekar

2026

EXECUTIVE SUMMARY

Sustainability is no longer an environmental aspiration. It is a structural economic transformation.

This Second Edition presents an integrated sustainability framework built upon four interdependent pillars:

1. Governance and Policy Architecture
2. Sustainable Finance and Capital Allocation
3. Technological Innovation and Industrial Transition
4. Behavioural and Cultural Transformation

The book positions sustainability not as sectoral reform, but as systemic redesign.

It explores:

- Circular economy implementation
- Extended Producer Responsibility (EPR) enforcement
- ESG regulatory transformation
- Climate finance evolution
- International environmental governance
- National legislative coordination
- Innovation ecosystems
- Sustainable consumption behaviour

The manuscript bridges:

- Academic theory
- Regulatory design
- Corporate governance
- Public policy
- Financial markets

It provides a structured roadmap for:

- Governments
- Regulators
- Financial institutions
- Corporations
- Academics
- Civil society

The Second Edition strengthens the policy dimension, incorporates global developments, and expands Malaysia's positioning within the regional sustainability landscape.

This book is designed as:

- A university reference text
- A policy handbook
- A corporate ESG guide
- A sustainability governance framework

It argues that environmental stability is inseparable from economic resilience.

The transition is not optional. It is structural.

INTRODUCTION

Second Edition (2026) - *Beyond Loving the Environment*

In line with providing factual and accurate information on the environment and sustainability to the members of the public particularly policymakers, regulators, academics, and industry leaders, this manuscript offers theoretical clarity, institutional guidance, and will instil greater awareness to the public at large on the environment and sustainability. Extreme weather events, weather related disasters, glacier retreats, threatened coastal areas, increased ocean acidity, heat waves, and changing animal and plant behaviour are signs of global warming. Our environment is changing for the worse. However, this situation can be improved if everyone is concerned and care deeply about global warming by implementing environmental friendly practices to safeguard the Earth for future generations. Sustainability is the capacity to endure.

In ecology the word describes how biological systems remain diverse and productive over time. Long-lived and healthy wetlands and forests are examples of sustainable biological systems. For humans, sustainability is the potential for long-term maintenance of wellbeing, which has ecological, economic, political and cultural dimensions. Preserving the environment is important to ensure a balance in our eco-system. The lush greenery we enjoy today will soon disappear if we do not take care of it. Everyone has a duty to protect, to preserve the environment and most importantly to love the environment including children. Therefore, the book "Beyond Loving the Environment" would serve to provide a platform of information and relevant materials that would enable members of the public to appreciate the environment and understand sustainability. Sustainability, Circular Economy, Climate Governance and Intergenerational Responsibility. From Awareness to Action: Sustainability, Circular Economy and Our Shared Future.

PART I

FOUNDATIONS OF ENVIRONMENTAL SYSTEMS

CHAPTER 1

THE INTERCONNECTED EARTH SYSTEM: UNDERSTANDING OUR PLANET AS A LIVING WHOLE

1.1 Introduction: From Isolated Problems to Systemic Thinking

Environmental challenges are often discussed as separate issues: climate change, deforestation, plastic pollution, biodiversity loss, water scarcity. Yet in reality, these are not isolated crises. They are symptoms of a deeper systemic imbalance within the Earth's interconnected systems.

The planet functions as a dynamic, integrated whole. Air currents influence oceans. Oceans regulate climate. Forests regulate atmospheric carbon. Soil fertility determines food security. Human activity now interacts with and increasingly disrupts each of these systems simultaneously.

To meaningfully address environmental degradation, we must move from fragmented thinking to systems thinking.

This chapter introduces the Earth System framework, the scientific foundation upon which modern sustainability policy is built.

1.2 The Four Major Earth Systems

Modern environmental science describes the planet through four primary interacting spheres:

1. The Atmosphere
2. The Hydrosphere
3. The Lithosphere
4. The Biosphere

Each system performs essential life-support functions.

1.2.1 The Atmosphere: The Planet's Protective Shield

The atmosphere is the thin layer of gases surrounding Earth. It regulates temperature, protects life from harmful solar radiation, and enables the hydrological cycle.

Key components include:

- Nitrogen (78%)
- Oxygen (21%)
- Trace gases including carbon dioxide, methane, and nitrous oxide

The balance of these gases determines climate stability.

However, since the Industrial Revolution, human activity primarily the burning of fossil fuels has increased atmospheric carbon dioxide concentrations to levels unprecedented in at least 800,000 years. This has altered radiative balance, strengthening the greenhouse effect.

The atmosphere is no longer merely a natural system it is a human influenced system.

1.2.2 The Hydrosphere: Water as a Regulating Force

The hydrosphere includes oceans, rivers, lakes, groundwater, glaciers, and atmospheric water vapour. It regulates climate, supports ecosystems, and sustains human civilization.

Oceans absorb approximately a quarter of anthropogenic carbon dioxide emissions. While this moderates atmospheric warming, it leads to ocean acidification threatening coral reefs, fisheries, and marine biodiversity.

Glacier retreat affects freshwater availability. Changes in ocean currents alter global weather patterns.

Water is not just a resource. It is a planetary stabilizer.

1.2.3 The Lithosphere: Earth's Physical Foundation

The lithosphere consists of the Earth's crust and upper mantle. It contains minerals, soils, fossil fuels, and critical materials essential for infrastructure and energy systems.

Human activity reshapes the lithosphere through:

- Mining
- Agriculture
- Urbanisation
- Infrastructure development

Land degradation, desertification, and soil erosion reduce agricultural productivity and threaten food security.

Healthy soils act as carbon sinks. Degraded soils release carbon.

Land management is climate policy.

1.2.4 The Biosphere: Life as a Regulating System

The biosphere encompasses all living organisms' plants, animals, microorganisms and the ecosystems they form.

Biodiversity is not aesthetic luxury. It is functional infrastructure.

Forests regulate carbon. Wetlands filter water. Pollinators sustain agriculture. Microorganisms decompose organic matter.

Current extinction rates are estimated to be tens to hundreds of times higher than natural background rates. Biodiversity loss weakens ecosystem resilience and reduces nature's capacity to buffer environmental shocks.

The biosphere is Earth's immune system. Its weakening threatens systemic collapse.

1.3 The Planetary Boundaries Framework

In 2009, Earth system scientists proposed the Planetary Boundaries framework to identify safe operating limits for humanity.

The framework identifies nine critical Earth system processes:

1. Climate change
2. Biodiversity loss
3. Biogeochemical flows (nitrogen & phosphorus cycles)
4. Land-system change
5. Freshwater use
6. Ocean acidification
7. Atmospheric aerosol loading
8. Ozone depletion
9. Novel entities (chemical pollution, plastics)

Several of these boundaries have already been transgressed.

This framework reframes sustainability as maintaining humanity within safe ecological limits.

1.4 The Anthropocene: A Human-Dominated Epoch

Scientists increasingly describe the present era as the Anthropocene a proposed geological epoch defined by human dominance over planetary systems.

Indicators include:

- Elevated carbon concentrations
- Plastic deposits in ocean sediments
- Widespread biodiversity decline
- Nitrogen cycle disruption due to synthetic fertilisers

Humanity is now a geological force.

This reality transforms environmental responsibility into a civilizational duty.

1.5 Interdependence and Feedback Loops

Earth systems operate through feedback mechanisms.

Positive feedback amplifies change:

- Melting ice reduces reflectivity (albedo), increasing warming.
- Thawing permafrost releases methane, accelerating warming.

Negative feedback stabilises systems:

- Increased plant growth absorbs more CO_2 (within limits).

When feedback loops intensify beyond thresholds, tipping points may occur.

Examples:

- Amazon rainforest dieback
- Greenland ice sheet collapse
- Coral reef ecosystem collapse

Crossing tipping points may lead to irreversible change.

1.6 Human Systems Within Earth Systems

Human economies depend entirely on ecological systems.

Energy production depends on geological resources. Agriculture depends on soil and water.

Industry depends on material extraction. Waste accumulates within ecosystems.

Traditional economic models treated nature as an externality.

Modern sustainability economics recognizes ecological limits as foundational constraints.

There is no economy outside ecology.

1.7 Policy Implications of Earth System Science

Understanding interconnected systems leads to several policy imperatives:

1. Integrated Governance

   Environmental ministries cannot operate in isolation from energy, finance, transport, or agriculture ministries.

2. Precautionary Principle

   When scientific uncertainty exists, preventive action should still be taken.

3. Intergenerational Equity

   Future generations have a right to ecological stability.

4. Systems-Based Regulation

   Climate, waste, land use, and water policies must align.

Fragmented policies produce unintended consequences.

1.8 Malaysia Within the Earth System Context

Malaysia is uniquely positioned within tropical biodiversity zones, marine corridors, and forest ecosystems.

National priorities must consider:

- Forest conservation as carbon strategy
- Marine ecosystem protection
- Flood management linked to land-use planning
- Urbanisation impacts on watershed systems

Sustainability policy must integrate national development goals with planetary boundaries.

1.9 From Awareness to Stewardship

Understanding Earth as an interconnected system transforms environmental protection from charity into stewardship.

We are not separate from nature. We are embedded within it.

Environmental degradation ultimately destabilizes human systems economically, socially, and politically.

Sustainability is not merely environmental preservation.

It is risk management for civilization.

1.10 Conclusion: The Foundation of All Sustainability Policy

The Earth system framework reveals three core truths:

1. Everything is interconnected.
2. Human activity now shapes planetary stability.
3. Sustainable governance requires systemic transformation.

This foundation prepares us to examine climate science in the next chapter not as an isolated issue, but as a systemic disruption within a delicately balanced planetary network.

Understanding the whole is the first step toward protecting it.

PART II

CLIMATE SCIENCE & CARBON GOVERNANCE

CHAPTER 2

CLIMATE CHANGE: SCIENTIFIC FOUNDATIONS AND GLOBAL IMPLICATIONS

2.1 Introduction: Climate as a Stabilising System

Climate is not simply "weather over time." It is a stabilising planetary system that regulates temperature, water cycles, seasonal patterns, ocean currents, and ecological balance. For approximately 10,000 years during the Holocene epoch the Earth's climate remained relatively stable. This climatic stability enabled agriculture, urbanisation, and the rise of civilisation.

Today, that stability is under threat.

Human-induced greenhouse gas emissions are altering atmospheric composition at a rate unprecedented in modern geological history. Climate change is not merely an environmental concern it is a structural risk to global stability, economic resilience, food security, and human health.

Understanding its scientific foundations is essential to designing effective policy.

2.2 The Greenhouse Effect: A Necessary but Delicate Balance

The greenhouse effect is a natural process. Without it, Earth's average surface temperature would be approximately −18°C rather than +15°C. Certain gases in the atmosphere trap outgoing infrared radiation, preventing heat from escaping into space.

The primary greenhouse gases include:

- Carbon dioxide (CO_2)
- Methane (CH_4)
- Nitrous oxide (N_2O)
- Water vapour
- Fluorinated gases (industrial origin)

The problem is not the existence of the greenhouse effect. The problem is its amplification.

Since the Industrial Revolution, fossil fuel combustion, deforestation, industrial processes, and intensive agriculture have significantly increased atmospheric concentrations of these gases.

This enhanced greenhouse effect leads to global warming.

2.3 Radiative Forcing and Energy Imbalance

Radiative forcing refers to the difference between incoming solar radiation and outgoing infrared radiation.

When greenhouse gases accumulate, they increase positive radiative forcing meaning more energy is retained within the Earth system.

Even a small imbalance in this global energy budget leads to large cumulative temperature changes over time.

Scientific measurements show that Earth is currently experiencing a persistent energy imbalance, meaning more heat is entering than leaving the system.

This excess energy manifests as:

- Rising global surface temperatures
- Ocean warming

- Ice sheet melting
- Increased atmospheric moisture

The climate system is accumulating heat.

2.4 Evidence of Climate Change

Climate science relies on multiple independent lines of evidence:

2.4.1 Temperature Records

Instrumental records show that global average temperatures have risen by more than 1°C above pre-industrial levels. The past decade has been the warmest in recorded history.

2.4.2 Ice Core Data

Ice cores extracted from Antarctica and Greenland contain trapped air bubbles that provide atmospheric records going back hundreds of thousands of years. Current CO_2 levels exceed historical natural fluctuations observed in these records.

2.4.3 Glacier and Ice Sheet Loss

Glaciers worldwide are retreating. The Greenland and Antarctic ice sheets are losing mass at accelerating rates, contributing to sea-level rise.

2.4.4 Ocean Warming and Acidification

Over 90% of excess heat from global warming is absorbed by oceans. Warmer oceans expand, contributing to sea-level rise. Simultaneously, absorbed CO_2 increases ocean acidity, threatening coral reefs and marine ecosystems.

2.4.5 Extreme Weather Events

Heatwaves, heavy rainfall events, droughts, and intense tropical cyclones are increasing in frequency and intensity. While weather variability always existed, climate change shifts probability distributions toward more extreme outcomes.

2.5 Tipping Points and Non-Linear Risks

Climate change is not a gradual linear process. It includes tipping elements thresholds beyond which changes become self-reinforcing and potentially irreversible.

Examples include:

- Arctic sea ice collapse
- Amazon rainforest dieback
- Permafrost methane release
- Atlantic Meridional Overturning Circulation weakening

Crossing tipping points could trigger cascading effects across multiple Earth systems.

This elevates climate change from environmental risk to systemic global risk.

2.6 The 1.5°C and 2°C Thresholds

International climate agreements focus on limiting global warming to:

- Well below 2°C
- Ideally 1.5°C above pre-industrial levels

Why does half a degree matter?

At 1.5°C:

- Coral reefs decline by 70–90%

At 2°C:

- Over 99% of coral reefs may be lost
- Extreme heat events increase substantially
- Sea-level rise accelerates

Small differences in temperature translate into large differences in impact.

2.7 Adaptation vs Mitigation

Climate policy operates on two primary fronts:

Mitigation

Reducing greenhouse gas emissions to limit warming.

Examples:

- Renewable energy transition
- Electrification of transport
- Energy efficiency improvements
- Reforestation
- Circular economy systems

Adaptation

Adjusting systems to cope with unavoidable impacts.

Examples:

- Flood-resistant infrastructure
- Heat-resilient urban design
- Drought-tolerant agriculture
- Coastal protection measures

Mitigation reduces future damage. Adaptation reduces current vulnerability. Both are necessary.

2.8 Climate Change and Southeast Asia

Southeast Asia is particularly vulnerable to climate impacts due to:

- Extensive coastlines
- Tropical storm exposure
- Agricultural dependence
- Rapid urbanisation

Projected impacts include:

- Increased flooding in coastal cities
- Higher intensity rainfall events
- Agricultural yield disruptions
- Marine ecosystem stress

For Malaysia, implications include:

- Increased flood frequency
- Coastal erosion
- Heat stress in urban areas
- Impacts on fisheries and palm oil production

Climate resilience must be integrated into national development planning.

2.9 Carbon Accounting and Emissions Scopes

Modern climate governance requires precise measurement.

Emissions are categorized as:

Scope 1 – Direct emissions from owned operations

Scope 2 – Indirect emissions from purchased electricity

Scope 3 – Indirect emissions across value chains

Scope 3 often represents the largest share of corporate emissions.

Accurate carbon accounting enables:

- Climate risk disclosure
- ESG reporting
- Regulatory compliance
- Carbon pricing participation

Measurement precedes management.

2.10 Climate Justice and Equity

Climate change raises ethical questions.

Those who contributed least to historical emissions often suffer the greatest impacts.

Developing nations face:

- Infrastructure vulnerabilities
- Financial constraints
- Climate adaptation burdens

This introduces the principle of "common but differentiated responsibilities" in international climate agreements.

Climate governance must balance environmental necessity with developmental equity.

2.11 Climate Risk as Financial Risk

Financial institutions increasingly recognize climate risk as systemic risk.

Physical risks:

- Flood damage
- Supply chain disruption
- Agricultural losses

Transition risks:

- Stranded fossil fuel assets
- Carbon regulation impacts
- Technology shifts

Climate change is now embedded within:

- Central bank risk frameworks
- Investor disclosure requirements
- Sustainability-linked finance

Environmental stability is financial stability.

2.12 The Urgency of Decarbonisation

To limit warming to 1.5°C, global emissions must decline rapidly within this decade and approach net-zero by mid-century.

Key transformation areas include:

- Power generation
- Transportation
- Industry
- Buildings
- Agriculture

Incremental adjustments are insufficient. Structural transformation is required.

2.13 Conclusion: Climate as the Defining Challenge of the Century

Climate change is not a future threat. It is a present reality reshaping environmental, economic, and political systems.

Scientific evidence is clear. The mechanisms are understood. The risks are escalating.

The central question is no longer whether climate change exists.

The question is whether governance systems can respond at the speed and scale required.

In the next chapter, we examine the carbon cycle and greenhouse gases in greater depth understanding how human activity disrupts the fundamental processes that regulate planetary temperature.

CHAPTER 3

THE CARBON CYCLE, GREENHOUSE GASES AND EMISSIONS PATHWAYS

3.1 Introduction: Carbon as the Currency of Life

Carbon is the foundational element of life. It forms the molecular backbone of plants, animals, microorganisms, and ecosystems. It is stored in forests, soils, oceans, rocks, and fossil fuels.

Under natural conditions, carbon circulates continuously between Earth systems through what is known as the carbon cycle.

For millions of years, this cycle maintained atmospheric balance. Human activity has now disrupted that equilibrium.

To understand climate governance, we must first understand the carbon system itself.

3.2 The Natural Carbon Cycle

The carbon cycle operates across three primary domains:

1. The atmosphere
2. The biosphere
3. The oceans and geosphere

3.2.1 Atmospheric Carbon

Carbon dioxide (CO_2) exists naturally in the atmosphere. It is absorbed by plants through photosynthesis and released through respiration and decomposition.

3.2.2 Biological Carbon

Through photosynthesis, plants convert CO_2 into biomass. Animals consume plants. When organisms die, carbon returns to the soil and atmosphere.

Forests function as carbon sinks when absorption exceeds release.

3.2.3 Oceanic Carbon

Oceans absorb large amounts of atmospheric CO_2. Some carbon dissolves in surface waters; some sinks to deep ocean layers through biological processes.

Marine phytoplankton play a critical role in carbon uptake.

3.2.4 Geological Carbon

Over millions of years, carbon becomes locked in:

- Sedimentary rocks
- Coal
- Oil
- Natural gas

These fossil carbon reserves were historically outside the short-term carbon cycle.

The industrial era reintroduced them into the atmosphere at accelerated rates.

3.3 Anthropogenic Disruption of the Carbon Cycle

Human activities have significantly altered carbon flows.

Primary sources include:

- Fossil fuel combustion
- Cement production
- Deforestation

- Agriculture
- Waste decomposition
- Industrial processes

Unlike natural carbon exchanges, fossil carbon emissions introduce additional carbon that was previously stored underground for millions of years.

The result is accumulation. Natural systems absorb roughly half of human emissions. The remainder accumulates in the atmosphere, increasing greenhouse gas concentrations.

3.4 Major Greenhouse Gases

While carbon dioxide is the dominant contributor to warming, other gases play critical roles.

3.4.1 Carbon Dioxide (CO_2)

Primary source: Fossil fuel combustion, land-use change

Atmospheric lifetime: Hundreds to thousands of years

Impact: Long-term warming driver

CO_2 is cumulative each emission adds to total atmospheric stock.

3.4.2 Methane (CH_4)

Primary source:

- Livestock (enteric fermentation)
- Landfills
- Rice cultivation
- Fossil fuel extraction leakage

Methane has a shorter atmospheric lifetime (approximately 12 years) but is far more potent than CO_2 over short time horizons.

Rapid methane reduction offers near term climate benefits.

3.4.3 Nitrous Oxide (N_2O)

Primary source:

- Agricultural fertilisers
- Industrial processes

Nitrous oxide has a long atmospheric lifetime and high global warming potential.

Agricultural intensification has significantly increased emissions.

3.4.4 Fluorinated Gases

Used in:

- Refrigeration
- Air-conditioning
- Industrial processes

These gases have extremely high warming potentials despite lower concentrations.

3.5 Carbon Budgets and Emissions Pathways

A carbon budget represents the total amount of CO_2 humanity can emit while limiting warming to a specific temperature threshold.

To limit warming to 1.5°C, the remaining global carbon budget is finite and rapidly shrinking.

Emissions pathways illustrate trajectories:

1. Business-as-usual (high emissions)
2. Gradual reduction
3. Rapid decarbonisation (net-zero by mid-century)

Only rapid decarbonisation aligns with safe climate thresholds.

Delay increases required reduction speed later raising economic and social disruption risks.

3.6 Land Use, Forestry, and Carbon Sinks

Forests and soils are vital carbon sinks.

Deforestation releases stored carbon and reduces future absorption capacity.

Tropical forests, including those in Southeast Asia, are particularly important due to:

- High biomass density
- High biodiversity
- Rapid growth rates

Sustainable land management practices include:

- Reforestation
- Agroforestry
- Mangrove restoration
- Peatland conservation

Peatlands are especially significant carbon stores. Their drainage for agriculture releases substantial emissions. Land-use policy is climate policy.

3.7 Agriculture and Methane Emissions

Agriculture contributes significantly to methane and nitrous oxide emissions.

Key drivers include:

- Cattle production
- Fertiliser application
- Rice paddies

Possible mitigation strategies:

- Improved feed efficiency
- Methane-reducing livestock supplements
- Precision fertiliser application
- Alternate wetting and drying in rice farming

Food systems must transition toward lower emission models without compromising food security.

3.8 Industrial Emissions and Hard-to-Abate Sectors

Certain sectors are particularly challenging to decarbonise:

- Steel production
- Cement manufacturing
- Aviation
- Shipping

These industries require:

- Green hydrogen
- Carbon capture and storage (CCS)
- Alternative materials
- Process innovation

Technological breakthroughs are necessary for full decarbonisation.

3.9 Carbon Removal and Negative Emissions

Even with rapid reductions, residual emissions may remain.

Carbon removal methods include:

- Afforestation
- Soil carbon sequestration

- Bioenergy with carbon capture and storage (BECCS)
- Direct air capture technologies

However, reliance on future removal carries risks:

- High cost
- Energy intensity
- Land competition
- Technological uncertainty

Mitigation remains more reliable than future removal.

3.10 Net-Zero: Definition and Misinterpretation

Net-zero does not mean zero emissions.

It means:

Total emissions – Total removals = Net-zero

However, net-zero targets must prioritize:

1. Absolute emission reductions
2. Limited reliance on offsets
3. Transparent carbon accounting

Poorly regulated carbon offsets risk greenwashing.

Integrity in carbon markets is essential.

3.11 Carbon Pricing and Market Mechanisms

Carbon pricing internalises environmental externalities.

Mechanisms include:

- Carbon taxes
- Emissions trading systems
- Cap-and-trade schemes

Pricing carbon signals economic actors to shift toward low-carbon alternatives.

Effective pricing requires:

- Accurate measurement
- Transparent reporting
- Strong regulatory oversight

3.12 Corporate Carbon Governance

Companies increasingly adopt:

- Science-based targets
- Net-zero commitments
- Scope 3 disclosure frameworks

Carbon governance is now integrated into:

- ESG reporting
- Investor decision-making
- Supply chain management

Corporate accountability is essential for national decarbonisation.

3.13 Malaysia's Carbon Context

Malaysia's emissions profile includes:

- Energy sector dominance
- Transport growth
- Industrial expansion
- Land-use change

Opportunities include:

- Renewable energy expansion
- Forest conservation
- Sustainable palm oil practices
- Methane reduction from landfills

Balancing economic development with emissions reduction is central to national climate strategy.

3.14 The Strategic Imperative of Rapid Transition

Delaying emissions reduction increases:

- Adaptation costs
- Disaster risk
- Financial instability
- Social inequity

Early action is economically rational.

Carbon transition is not anti-development.

It is development redefined.

3.15 Conclusion: Carbon Governance as Civilisational Responsibility

The carbon cycle once operated in balance for millennia.

Humanity has altered it within two centuries.

Stabilising the climate requires:

- Scientific understanding
- Political will
- Economic transformation
- Institutional integrity

Carbon governance is not solely environmental management.

It is the restructuring of the global economy to align with ecological reality.

In the next chapter, we move from carbon to energy systems examining the transition from fossil fuels to renewable energy and the infrastructure shifts required.

CHAPTER 4

ENERGY TRANSITION: FOSSIL FUELS, RENEWABLES AND INFRASTRUCTURE TRANSFORMATION

4.1 Introduction: Energy as the Engine of Modern Civilization

Energy underpins every modern system:

- Electricity generation
- Transportation
- Industrial production
- Urban infrastructure
- Digital networks

The Industrial Revolution was powered by coal. The 20th century was driven by oil and natural gas. The 21st century must be defined by clean energy transition.

Energy systems are responsible for the majority of global greenhouse gas emissions. Decarbonising energy is therefore the central pillar of climate mitigation.

But energy transition is not merely technological replacement. It is infrastructure transformation at civilisational scale.

4.2 Fossil Fuels: Benefits, Legacy and Risks

Fossil fuels enabled:

- Industrial growth
- Medical advancements
- Agricultural productivity
- Mass transportation
- Economic expansion

They remain energy-dense, transportable, and historically cost-effective.

However, their continued use produces:

- Carbon dioxide emissions
- Methane leakage
- Air pollution
- Environmental degradation

Beyond climate impacts, fossil fuel combustion contributes to respiratory illness and premature mortality.

The energy transition must therefore address both climate and public health imperatives.

4.3 Stranded Assets and Economic Transition Risk

Energy transition creates financial implications.

Stranded assets refer to fossil fuel infrastructure and reserves that may lose economic value due to:

- Climate regulations
- Carbon pricing
- Technological disruption
- Investor withdrawal

Coal plants, oil reserves, and gas infrastructure risk becoming economically unviable before the end of their expected operational life.

This creates transition risk for:

- Energy companies
- Pension funds
- Financial institutions
- National economies dependent on fossil exports

Planned transition reduces systemic economic shocks.

4.4 Renewable Energy Technologies

Renewable energy sources generate electricity without direct greenhouse gas emissions.

4.4.1 Solar Energy

Photovoltaic (PV) panels convert sunlight into electricity.

Advantages:

- Rapid cost decline
- Modular deployment
- Suitable for rooftops and utility-scale farms

Challenges:

- Intermittency
- Land use considerations
- Storage requirements

4.4.2 Wind Energy

Wind turbines harness kinetic energy from moving air.

Onshore wind is now cost-competitive in many regions.

Offshore wind offers high capacity factors but requires greater capital investment.

4.4.3 Hydropower

Hydropower provides stable baseload electricity but may involve ecological and social displacement risks if not carefully managed.

4.4.4 Biomass and Bioenergy

Bioenergy uses organic material for power generation.

Sustainability depends on:

- Responsible sourcing
- Avoiding deforestation
- Lifecycle emissions assessment

4.4.5 Geothermal Energy

Geothermal systems harness underground heat.

Suitable in regions with geological activity, though initial capital costs can be high.

4.5 Energy Storage and Grid Modernisation

Renewable energy integration requires:

- Battery storage systems
- Pumped hydro storage
- Smart grid technologies
- Demand response systems

Electricity grids must evolve from centralised fossil based generation to decentralised renewable networks.

Digitalisation enables:

- Real-time monitoring
- Load balancing
- Consumer participation

Grid resilience is a core component of energy security.

4.6 Electrification of Transport

Transport contributes significantly to emissions.

Energy transition includes:

- Electric vehicles (EVs)
- Electrified public transport
- Charging infrastructure expansion

Benefits include:

- Reduced urban air pollution
- Lower operating costs
- Integration with renewable energy

However, EV sustainability depends on:

- Battery material sourcing
- Renewable electricity supply
- Recycling systems

Transport transition must integrate circular economy principles.

4.7 Green Hydrogen and Industrial Decarbonisation

Certain sectors cannot easily electrify.

Green hydrogen produced using renewable electricity offers solutions for:

- Steel production
- Chemical manufacturing
- Heavy transport
- Aviation fuels

Hydrogen infrastructure development is capital-intensive but strategically important.

Industrial decarbonisation is essential for achieving net-zero.

4.8 Energy Efficiency: The Invisible Resource

Energy efficiency is often the most cost-effective climate strategy.

Examples include:

- Efficient buildings
- LED lighting
- Industrial optimisation
- Smart appliances

Reducing demand lowers required supply expansion.

Efficiency is the fastest emission reduction pathway available.

4.9 Energy Justice and Just Transition

Energy transition must consider social equity.

A just transition ensures:

- Worker retraining in fossil-dependent sectors
- Affordable energy access

- Community inclusion in renewable development
- Avoidance of energy poverty

Transition cannot create new inequalities while solving environmental problems.

Policy design must balance environmental ambition with social fairness.

4.10 Southeast Asia and Energy Transition

Southeast Asia faces dual pressures:

- Rapid economic growth
- Rising energy demand

Coal expansion historically supported growth. However, renewable energy potential is significant, particularly solar.

Malaysia's energy strategy includes:

- Increasing renewable share
- Enhancing grid infrastructure
- Improving energy efficiency standards

Balancing industrial competitiveness with climate commitments remains central to policy.

4.11 Policy Instruments for Energy Transition

Governments deploy multiple tools:

- Renewable energy targets
- Feed-in tariffs
- Carbon pricing
- Fossil fuel subsidy reform
- Green finance incentives
- Public-private partnerships

Policy certainty encourages investment.

Regulatory instability deters capital flows.

4.12 The Role of Private Sector and Finance

Financial institutions increasingly align portfolios with:

- Net-zero pathways
- Sustainable finance taxonomies
- ESG integration

Capital allocation shapes energy infrastructure outcomes.

Green bonds and sustainability-linked loans fund renewable expansion.

Transition is not only technological it is financial.

4.13 Infrastructure Resilience and Climate Adaptation

Energy infrastructure must withstand climate impacts.

Extreme weather events threaten:

- Transmission lines
- Power plants
- Coastal facilities

Resilient infrastructure reduces future repair costs and system disruptions.

Energy security now includes climate resilience.

4.14 The Strategic Imperative

Energy systems define economic structure.

Transitioning away from fossil fuels:

- Reduces climate risk
- Enhances energy independence
- Stimulates innovation
- Creates employment in emerging sectors

Delay increases cumulative emissions and transition costs.

Proactive transformation is economically rational.

4.15 Conclusion: From Extraction to Regeneration

The fossil fuel era was built on extraction.

The renewable era must be built on regeneration.

Energy transition represents:

- Technological innovation
- Financial restructuring
- Policy coordination
- Cultural transformation

It is not a single project but a multi-decade reconfiguration of global infrastructure.

The next chapter shifts from energy to material systems examining how production and consumption patterns generate waste, and how circular economy models offer systemic solutions.

CHAPTER 5

FROM LINEAR TO CIRCULAR: RETHINKING PRODUCTION AND CONSUMPTION

5.1 Introduction: The Problem of the Linear Economy

Modern industrial development has largely followed a linear model:

Extract → Produce → Consume → Dispose

This model assumes:

- Infinite resources
- Unlimited waste absorption capacity
- Low environmental cost

For decades, it delivered economic growth and consumer abundance. However, it also produced:

- Resource depletion
- Pollution accumulation
- Landfill expansion
- Ocean plastic contamination
- Climate emissions from production and disposal

The linear economy externalises environmental cost.

The circular economy internalises it.

5.2 Material Extraction and Resource Pressure

Global material extraction has increased dramatically over the past century.

Key material categories include:

- Biomass
- Fossil fuels
- Metals
- Non-metallic minerals

Rapid urbanisation, infrastructure expansion, and consumer culture have accelerated resource demand.

Consequences include:

- Deforestation
- Habitat destruction
- Water pollution
- Carbon emissions from mining and processing

Material throughput is directly linked to environmental degradation.

5.3 Waste as a Systemic Design Failure

Waste is often treated as an end-of-pipe issue a problem of disposal.

However, waste originates at the design stage.

Products are frequently designed:

- For single use
- With mixed materials difficult to separate
- Without repairability
- Without recycling compatibility

Waste is therefore not merely a management problem.

It is a design problem.

5.4 The Circular Economy Framework

The circular economy reimagines production systems by prioritising:

1. Design out waste and pollution
2. Keep products and materials in use
3. Regenerate natural systems

Instead of linear flow, circular systems operate in loops.

Materials circulate through:

- Reuse
- Repair
- Refurbishment
- Remanufacturing
- Recycling

Biological materials return safely to ecosystems. Technical materials remain within industrial cycles.

5.5 Linear vs Circular Economy: Structural Comparison

Linear Model

- High extraction
- Short product lifespans
- Landfill accumulation
- Resource volatility
- Pollution externalities

Circular Model

- Reduced virgin extraction
- Extended product life
- Industrial symbiosis

- Resource efficiency
- Lower emissions

Circularity enhances both environmental and economic resilience.

5.6 Economic Benefits of Circularity

Circular systems offer:

- Reduced material costs
- Supply chain stability
- Innovation opportunities
- New employment sectors
- Lower waste management costs

Business models shift from product ownership to service provision:

- Leasing
- Product-as-a-service
- Take-back schemes
- Repair services

Circular economy is not anti-growth. It is growth decoupled from material depletion.

5.7 Industrial Symbiosis

Industrial symbiosis involves:

- One company's waste becoming another's resource

Examples include:

- Waste heat reuse
- By-product exchange
- Shared logistics infrastructure

This reduces raw material demand and waste generation simultaneously.

Industrial ecosystems mirror natural ecosystems where outputs become inputs.

5.8 Design for Circularity

Design principles include:

- Modular components
- Standardised parts
- Easy disassembly
- Durable materials
- Recyclable material selection

Product passports and material tracking systems enhance transparency.

Circular design begins before production.

5.9 Waste Hierarchy and Policy Alignment

The waste hierarchy ranks waste management priorities:

1. Prevention
2. Reduction
3. Reuse
4. Recycling
5. Recovery
6. Disposal

Effective policy prioritises prevention over disposal.

Landfilling is the least desirable option.

Circular policy instruments include:

- Extended Producer Responsibility (EPR)
- Deposit-return systems
- Mandatory recycling targets
- Eco-design regulations

Policy must incentivise circular behaviour.

5.10 Plastics and Marine Pollution

Plastic production has grown exponentially.

Challenges include:

- Single-use packaging
- Microplastic contamination
- Ocean debris accumulation
- Low global recycling rates

Circular solutions include:

- Refillable systems
- Biodegradable alternatives (with caution)
- Recycled content mandates
- Producer responsibility schemes

Plastic pollution is a visible symbol of linear system failure.

5.11 Urbanisation and Construction Waste

Construction and demolition waste represent major material flows.

Circular approaches include:

- Recycled aggregates
- Modular construction

- Building material recovery
- Adaptive reuse of buildings

Urban design must integrate circular material flows.

Cities are resource hubs not just consumption centers.

5.12 Food Waste and Organic Circularity

Food waste contributes to:

- Methane emissions
- Resource inefficiency
- Water waste

Circular solutions include:

- Improved supply chain management
- Consumer education
- Composting systems
- Anaerobic digestion

Organic waste can generate biogas and fertiliser.

Food circularity strengthens climate mitigation.

5.13 Measuring Circularity

Circularity metrics include:

- Material circularity indicators
- Recycling rates
- Waste diversion rates
- Resource productivity ratios

Accurate measurement enables:

- Policy evaluation
- Corporate reporting
- Investment decisions

Data transparency supports accountability.

5.14 **Malaysia and Circular Economy Transition**

Malaysia's circular transition priorities include:

- Plastic waste reduction
- Strengthening recycling systems
- EPR implementation
- Sustainable packaging standards
- Waste-to-energy considerations

Regional cooperation is essential due to transboundary waste flows.

Circular economy development must align with national industrial strategy.

5.15 **Barriers to Circular Implementation**

Common barriers include:

- Low virgin material costs
- Limited recycling infrastructure
- Consumer behaviour patterns
- Regulatory gaps
- Financing challenges

Overcoming these barriers requires:

- Policy coherence
- Financial incentives
- Industry collaboration
- Public awareness

Transition is systemic, not incremental.

5.16 Circular Economy and Climate Mitigation

Material production contributes significantly to global emissions.

Reducing material demand through circularity:

- Lowers energy consumption
- Reduces extraction emissions
- Minimises landfill methane
- Enhances carbon efficiency

Circular economy is therefore a climate strategy.

5.17 Conclusion: Designing a Regenerative Economy

The linear economy was efficient at production.

The circular economy must be efficient at preservation.

It demands:

- Systems thinking
- Policy reform
- Business innovation
- Consumer participation

Circularity is not optional in a resource-constrained world.

It represents the structural redesign of economic systems to operate within planetary limits.

In the next chapter, we deepen the discussion of waste governance focusing specifically on Extended Producer Responsibility (EPR) as a regulatory instrument for systemic transformation.

CHAPTER 6

EXTENDED PRODUCER RESPONSIBILITY (EPR): LEGAL ARCHITECTURE AND IMPLEMENTATION

6.1 Introduction: From Voluntary Action to Legal Obligation

Circular economy principles require structural enforcement mechanisms. One of the most powerful regulatory instruments developed in recent decades is Extended Producer Responsibility (EPR).

EPR shifts responsibility for post-consumer waste management from governments and taxpayers to producers those who place products and packaging onto the market.

Under EPR frameworks, producers are financially and/or physically responsible for:

- Collection
- Recycling
- Treatment
- Environmentally sound disposal

EPR transforms waste from a municipal burden into a producer-managed lifecycle responsibility.

6.2 The Policy Logic Behind EPR

Traditional waste systems operate as public services funded by taxation.

This creates two distortions:

1. Producers lack incentives to design recyclable or reusable products.
2. Waste management costs are externalised to society.

EPR corrects this by:

- Internalising end-of-life costs into product pricing.
- Encouraging eco-design.
- Reducing material complexity.
- Increasing recyclability.

The policy principle is simple:

Those who profit from placing products on the market must also manage their environmental impact.

6.3 Core Elements of EPR Systems

Effective EPR frameworks include several structural components:

6.3.1 Obligated Producers

Manufacturers, importers, or brand owners placing products or packaging on the domestic market.

6.3.2 Producer Responsibility Organisations (PROs)

Collective entities that manage compliance on behalf of producers, including:

- Collection systems
- Recycling contracts
- Reporting obligations

6.3.3 Collection and Recovery Targets

Governments set legally binding:

- Recycling rate targets
- Recovery rate targets
- Recycled content requirements

6.3.4 Reporting and Transparency

Producers must declare:

- Volume placed on market (POM)
- Material composition
- Recovery performance

Accurate reporting underpins system credibility.

6.4 Financial Mechanisms

EPR systems typically operate through:

- Eco-modulated fees (fees based on recyclability or environmental impact)
- Weight-based contributions
- Deposit-return schemes (for beverage containers)
- Advanced recycling fees

Eco-modulation incentivises:

- Recyclable packaging
- Reduced material complexity
- Lower carbon intensity materials

Well-designed fee structures influence product design decisions.

6.5 EPR and Circular Design Incentives

EPR creates design pressure in multiple ways:

- Non-recyclable materials incur higher fees.
- Mixed-material packaging becomes economically inefficient.
- Reusable systems may receive fee exemptions.

Over time, producers adapt to minimise compliance costs by redesigning products.

EPR therefore shifts design norms across industries.

6.6 Sectors Commonly Covered by EPR

EPR frameworks typically apply to:

- Packaging waste
- Electrical and electronic equipment (WEEE)
- Batteries
- Tyres
- Vehicles
- Plastics
- Textiles (in emerging frameworks)

Packaging EPR is often the entry point due to high waste volumes.

6.7 Deposit-Return Systems (DRS)

Deposit-return systems complement EPR.

Consumers pay a small deposit when purchasing beverage containers and receive it back upon return.

Benefits include:

- High collection rates
- Reduced litter
- High-quality recyclate
- Consumer participation

DRS demonstrates how behavioural economics supports environmental policy.

6.8 Governance Challenges in EPR Implementation

EPR systems face common challenges:

- Free riders (non-compliant producers)
- Underreporting of volumes
- Informal sector integration
- Administrative capacity constraints
- Enforcement weaknesses

Robust regulatory oversight is essential.

Digital reporting systems improve compliance monitoring.

6.9 Integrating the Informal Sector

In many developing economies, informal waste collectors play significant roles in recycling systems.

Effective EPR implementation should:

- Formalise and integrate informal workers
- Provide safety protections
- Ensure fair compensation
- Avoid displacement without alternatives

Social inclusion strengthens environmental outcomes.

6.10 EPR as Economic Instrument, Not Taxation

EPR is not intended as revenue generation.

Its objective is:

- Waste reduction
- Recycling efficiency
- Design transformation

Funds collected must be transparently allocated toward waste management systems.

Public trust depends on accountability.

6.11 EPR and Climate Mitigation

EPR contributes to climate mitigation by:

- Reducing landfill methane
- Increasing material recovery
- Reducing virgin material production emissions
- Encouraging low-carbon design

Material recycling often consumes less energy than primary extraction.

EPR aligns waste governance with climate policy.

6.12 Malaysia and EPR Development

Malaysia has been progressively developing EPR frameworks, particularly for packaging and plastics.

Key strategic priorities include:

- Establishing clear regulatory obligations
- Strengthening Producer Responsibility Organisations
- Developing national recycling infrastructure

- Ensuring data transparency
- Encouraging eco-design standards

EPR supports Malaysia's broader circular economy roadmap and sustainability commitments.

Effective implementation requires:

- Inter-ministerial coordination
- Industry engagement
- Public awareness campaigns

6.13 Measuring EPR Effectiveness

Key performance indicators include:

- Collection rates
- Recycling rates
- Recycled content percentages
- Reduction in landfill volumes
- Compliance rates
- Design improvements

Continuous review and regulatory refinement ensure system improvement.

6.14 Risks of Poorly Designed EPR Systems

Without strong governance, EPR can face:

- Fee misallocation
- Greenwashing
- Inadequate infrastructure investment
- Market distortions
- Export of waste to weaker regulatory jurisdictions

International cooperation and transparency reduce these risks.

6.15 EPR in the Context of ESG and Corporate Governance

EPR compliance increasingly intersects with ESG reporting.

Companies must disclose:

- Packaging footprints
- Recycling performance
- Waste reduction strategies
- Lifecycle impacts

Investors evaluate waste governance as part of sustainability risk assessments.

EPR is now both regulatory and reputational.

6.16 Strategic Importance of EPR

EPR achieves three systemic objectives:

1. Financial internalisation of waste costs
2. Design transformation incentives
3. Infrastructure funding stability

It shifts waste management from reactive disposal to proactive lifecycle management.

EPR operationalises circular economy principles through law.

6.17 Conclusion: Responsibility Beyond Production

The traditional model separated production from waste.

EPR reunites them.

By extending responsibility beyond the point of sale, EPR transforms:

- Corporate accountability
- Product design
- Material recovery
- Consumer behaviour

It represents a fundamental shift in environmental governance from voluntary sustainability to legally structured responsibility.

In the next chapter, we expand into ESG (Environmental, Social, and Governance) frameworks examining how sustainability performance is measured, disclosed, and integrated into corporate and financial decision-making.

CHAPTER 7

ESG: ENVIRONMENTAL, SOCIAL AND GOVERNANCE IN THE ERA OF SUSTAINABLE FINANCE

7.1 Introduction: From Corporate Social Responsibility to ESG Accountability

For decades, corporate sustainability was framed as Corporate Social Responsibility (CSR) largely voluntary, philanthropic, and peripheral to core business operations.

Today, sustainability has moved from the margins to the balance sheet.

Environmental, Social and Governance (ESG) frameworks now influence:

- Capital allocation
- Investor decisions
- Credit ratings
- Regulatory compliance
- Corporate valuations

ESG is no longer reputational branding. It is risk management and fiduciary responsibility.

7.2 The Evolution of ESG

The rise of ESG reflects three converging developments:

1. Recognition of climate and environmental risk as financial risk
2. Investor demand for transparency and long-term value protection
3. Regulatory expansion of sustainability disclosure requirements

Institutional investors increasingly assess whether companies are resilient to environmental disruption, regulatory change, and social instability.

Sustainability performance now influences cost of capital.

7.3 The Three Pillars of ESG

7.3.1 Environmental (E)

Environmental criteria assess how a company interacts with natural systems.

Key indicators include:

- Greenhouse gas emissions (Scopes 1, 2, 3)
- Energy efficiency
- Renewable energy use
- Waste management practices
- Water stewardship
- Biodiversity impact
- Pollution control

Environmental risk exposure affects long-term profitability.

7.3.2 **Social (S)**

Social criteria evaluate relationships with:

- Employees
- Suppliers
- Customers
- Communities

Key metrics include:

- Labour standards
- Workplace safety
- Diversity and inclusion
- Supply chain ethics
- Human rights compliance
- Community engagement

Social instability can disrupt operations and damage brand trust.

7.3.3 **Governance (G)**

Governance assesses corporate leadership and accountability.

Key indicators include:

- Board structure and independence
- Executive remuneration alignment
- Anti-corruption measures
- Transparency in reporting
- Risk management frameworks

Weak governance amplifies environmental and social risks.

7.4 ESG and Climate Risk Disclosure

Climate risk disclosure is becoming mandatory in many jurisdictions.

Disclosure frameworks require companies to assess:

- Physical risks (flooding, heatwaves, supply disruption)
- Transition risks (carbon pricing, regulatory changes)
- Scenario analysis under different warming pathways

Transparent reporting reduces information asymmetry between companies and investors.

Climate disclosure enhances market efficiency.

7.5 Sustainable Finance Instruments

The integration of ESG has catalysed new financial instruments:

- Green bonds
- Sustainability-linked loans
- Transition bonds
- ESG-linked equity funds

Green bonds finance projects such as:

- Renewable energy
- Energy efficiency
- Waste management infrastructure
- Clean transport

Sustainability-linked loans tie interest rates to ESG performance targets.

Finance is increasingly conditional upon measurable sustainability progress.

7.6 ESG Ratings and Standardisation Challenges

Multiple ESG rating agencies evaluate corporate performance.

However, challenges include:

- Methodological differences
- Data inconsistencies
- Varying materiality definitions
- Greenwashing risks

The absence of global standardisation complicates comparability.

Efforts toward harmonised sustainability reporting standards are expanding.

7.7 Greenwashing and Integrity Risks

Greenwashing occurs when companies exaggerate sustainability claims without substantive action.

Risks include:

- Misleading environmental claims
- Selective disclosure
- Reliance on weak carbon offsets
- Inflated ESG ratings

Strong governance, regulatory enforcement, and third-party verification reduce greenwashing risks.

Credibility is central to ESG legitimacy.

7.8 ESG and Regulatory Expansion

Governments are increasingly mandating ESG disclosures.

Policy drivers include:

- Climate commitments
- Financial system stability
- Investor protection
- Consumer transparency

Mandatory reporting enhances accountability.

Voluntary disclosure is gradually being replaced by regulated frameworks.

7.9 ESG and Supply Chain Accountability

Global supply chains create extended environmental and social risks.

Companies are now expected to monitor:

- Upstream emissions
- Raw material sourcing
- Labour practices in supplier facilities
- Human rights risks

Scope 3 emissions reporting has expanded ESG responsibility beyond direct operations.

Supply chain transparency is becoming a competitive differentiator.

7.10 ESG Integration into Corporate Strategy

Leading firms integrate ESG into:

- Board-level governance
- Risk management systems
- Capital expenditure planning
- Executive performance metrics

ESG must align with core business strategy.

Sustainability cannot remain a compliance department function.

7.11 ESG and Small and Medium Enterprises (SMEs)

While large corporations dominate ESG discussions, SMEs face increasing expectations through:

- Supply chain requirements
- Bank financing conditions
- Government procurement standards

Capacity building and phased implementation are essential to avoid disproportionate burdens.

Inclusive ESG frameworks support economic stability.

7.12 ESG in Emerging Economies

Emerging markets face:

- Infrastructure financing needs
- Development pressures
- Resource dependence

Balancing growth with ESG expectations requires:

- Policy coherence
- Financial support mechanisms
- Technical assistance
- International cooperation

ESG must be contextualised within development realities.

7.13 Malaysia and ESG Evolution

Malaysia's ESG development includes:

- Sustainable finance frameworks
- Corporate governance codes
- Climate-related disclosures
- Green sukuk (Islamic green bonds) initiatives
- Bursa sustainability reporting requirements

Financial institutions are integrating sustainability risk assessment into lending decisions.

National competitiveness increasingly depends on ESG credibility.

7.14 ESG as Systemic Risk Management

Environmental degradation, social inequality, and governance failures create systemic instability.

ESG addresses:

- Climate transition risk
- Resource scarcity
- Social unrest
- Regulatory unpredictability

Strong ESG performance reduces long-term volatility.

Sustainability is financial prudence.

7.15 Limitations of ESG

Despite progress, ESG faces limitations:

- Data gaps
- Overemphasis on disclosure over impact
- Risk of box-ticking compliance
- Short-term market pressures

True sustainability requires real operational transformation not merely reporting sophistication.

7.16 Linking ESG, EPR and Circular Economy

ESG frameworks intersect directly with:

- Carbon governance
- Extended Producer Responsibility
- Circular design standards
- Waste reduction targets

Environmental metrics now require lifecycle transparency.

ESG provides the financial lens. EPR provides the regulatory mechanism.

Circular economy provides the design framework.

Together, they reshape industrial systems.

7.17 Conclusion: Sustainability as Fiduciary Duty

The era of voluntary sustainability narratives is ending.

Investors, regulators, and consumers demand:

- Measurable impact
- Transparent disclosure
- Accountable governance

ESG embeds environmental and social considerations into financial decision-making.

It aligns capital markets with planetary boundaries.

In the next chapter, we examine biodiversity and ecosystem services understanding how natural capital underpins economic systems and why its preservation is central to sustainability governance.

CHAPTER 8

BIODIVERSITY, NATURAL CAPITAL AND ECOSYSTEM SERVICES

8.1 Introduction: Nature as Infrastructure

Economic systems are often viewed as independent of natural systems. Yet every sector: agriculture, energy, construction, manufacturing, finance ultimately depends on ecological stability.

Forests regulate climate. Wetlands filter water. Mangroves protect coastlines. Pollinators sustain food production.

Nature performs essential services without formal pricing mechanisms. When these services degrade, economic systems incur hidden costs.

Biodiversity loss is not merely ecological decline. It is infrastructure erosion.

8.2 Defining Biodiversity

Biodiversity refers to the variability of life at three levels:

1. Genetic diversity
2. Species diversity
3. Ecosystem diversity

Each level contributes to resilience.

High biodiversity strengthens ecosystem stability under stress.

Low biodiversity increases vulnerability to collapse.

Diverse systems recover faster from disturbances.

8.3 Drivers of Biodiversity Loss

Global biodiversity decline is driven by:

- Land-use change (deforestation, urbanisation)
- Overexploitation (overfishing, hunting)
- Pollution
- Climate change
- Invasive species

Habitat destruction remains the dominant driver.

Agricultural expansion and infrastructure development fragment ecosystems, reducing species viability.

8.4 Ecosystem Services Framework

Ecosystem services classify the benefits humans derive from nature into four categories:

8.4.1 Provisioning Services

Food

- Freshwater
- Timber
- Medicinal resources

8.4.2 Regulating Services

Climate regulation

- Flood control
- Water purification
- Disease control

8.4.3 Supporting Services

Nutrient cycling

- Soil formation
- Photosynthesis

8.4.4 Cultural Services

Recreation

- Spiritual value
- Tourism
- Cultural identity

Economic systems depend on all four categories.

8.5 Natural Capital: Valuing Ecological Assets

Natural capital refers to the stock of natural resources and ecosystems that generate ecosystem services.

Examples include:

- Forest carbon storage
- Fisheries biomass
- Watershed protection systems
- Coral reef ecosystems

Natural capital accounting attempts to measure:

- Economic value of ecosystem services
- Depletion rates
- Restoration costs

Integrating natural capital into national accounts aligns economic planning with ecological limits.

8.6 Biodiversity and Climate Interdependence

Climate change and biodiversity loss are mutually reinforcing.

Warming temperatures alter habitats. Habitat destruction reduces carbon sequestration capacity.

Forests and oceans act as carbon sinks. Their degradation accelerates climate change.

Protecting biodiversity supports climate mitigation.

Nature-based solutions provide dual benefits.

8.7 Deforestation and Land Degradation

Forests are critical biodiversity reservoirs and carbon sinks.

Deforestation leads to:

- Habitat loss
- Carbon emissions
- Soil erosion
- Hydrological disruption

Land degradation reduces agricultural productivity and increases vulnerability to drought.

Sustainable land management integrates conservation with economic activity.

8.8 Marine Biodiversity and Ocean Health

Oceans provide:

- Fisheries
- Climate regulation
- Oxygen production
- Coastal protection

Marine threats include:

- Overfishing
- Coral bleaching
- Plastic pollution
- Ocean acidification

Coral reef degradation threatens food security and tourism economies.

Marine protected areas improve ecosystem recovery.

8.9 **Pollinators and Food Security**

Pollinators such as bees, butterflies, and birds are essential for crop production.

Declining pollinator populations threaten:

- Fruit production
- Vegetable supply
- Nutritional diversity

Agricultural sustainability depends on biodiversity protection.

Monoculture expansion increases ecological vulnerability.

8.10 **Urban Biodiversity**

Urban environments often neglect ecological planning.

However, green infrastructure provides:

- Heat mitigation
- Air purification
- Flood absorption
- Mental health benefits

Urban biodiversity strategies include:

- Green corridors
- Tree canopy expansion
- Wetland restoration
- Permeable surfaces

Cities must integrate ecological resilience into planning frameworks.

8.11 Biodiversity and Economic Risk

Loss of biodiversity creates systemic risk:

- Supply chain disruptions
- Agricultural instability
- Increased disaster vulnerability
- Tourism decline

Investors increasingly assess biodiversity exposure.

Natural capital degradation affects financial performance.

8.12 Policy Instruments for Biodiversity Protection

Governments deploy:

- Protected area designation
- Land-use zoning
- Environmental impact assessments
- Biodiversity offsets
- Restoration mandates
- Conservation incentives

Policy effectiveness depends on enforcement capacity and community engagement.

Conservation cannot succeed without local participation.

8.13 Indigenous Knowledge and Stewardship

Indigenous communities often maintain long-standing ecological knowledge systems.

Their stewardship practices include:

- Sustainable harvesting
- Rotational land management
- Forest guardianship

Integrating indigenous knowledge strengthens biodiversity governance.

Equitable benefit-sharing promotes conservation incentives.

8.14 Biodiversity Finance

Emerging financial mechanisms include:

- Biodiversity credits
- Conservation funds
- Payment for ecosystem services
- Blended finance models

Mobilising private capital for conservation is increasingly necessary.

Public funding alone is insufficient to address global biodiversity loss.

8.15 Malaysia as a Biodiversity Hotspot

Malaysia is one of the world's biodiversity-rich nations, with:

- Tropical rainforests
- Coral reefs
- Mangrove ecosystems
- Unique endemic species

Economic sectors such as palm oil, timber, fisheries, and tourism intersect directly with biodiversity.

Balancing development and conservation is a strategic national priority.

Forest conservation supports:

- Climate commitments
- Tourism revenue
- Ecosystem stability

National biodiversity policy must align with economic planning.

8.16 Nature-Based Solutions (NbS)

Nature-based solutions address environmental challenges using ecosystem restoration.

Examples include:

- Mangrove restoration for coastal protection
- Reforestation for carbon sequestration
- Wetland restoration for flood mitigation

NbS offer cost-effective climate adaptation and mitigation strategies.

They require long-term stewardship and monitoring.

8.17 Measuring Biodiversity Performance

Indicators include:

- Species population trends
- Habitat coverage
- Deforestation rates
- Protected area percentages
- Ecosystem health indices

Corporate biodiversity reporting is expanding under ESG frameworks.

Measurement enhances accountability.

8.18 Conclusion: Protecting Life-Support Systems

Biodiversity is not a peripheral environmental concern.

It is the foundation of food systems, climate regulation, water security, and economic stability.

The degradation of natural capital undermines long-term development.

Sustainability requires:

- Ecological preservation
- Economic alignment
- Policy enforcement
- Community participation

Nature is not external to economic systems.

It is the system within which economies operate.

In the next chapter, we examine water systems and freshwater governance exploring how hydrological stability underpins environmental and societal resilience.

CHAPTER 9

WATER SECURITY, HYDROLOGICAL CYCLES AND RESOURCE GOVERNANCE

9.1 Introduction: Water as the Foundation of Civilisation

Water sustains:

- Human survival
- Agriculture
- Industry
- Energy production
- Ecosystem health

No society can function without stable water systems. Historically, civilisations flourished near rivers and declined when water systems collapsed.

Despite covering over 70% of the planet's surface, less than 1% of Earth's water is readily accessible freshwater suitable for human use.

Water scarcity, contamination, and mismanagement now pose major global risks.

Water governance is therefore a core pillar of sustainability.

9.2 The Hydrological Cycle: A Delicate Circulation System

The hydrological cycle describes the continuous movement of water through:

- Evaporation
- Condensation
- Precipitation
- Infiltration
- Runoff
- Groundwater recharge

This cycle regulates climate, soil moisture, and freshwater availability.

Climate change intensifies the cycle:

- Increased evaporation
- Heavier rainfall events
- Prolonged droughts

Hydrological instability directly affects food security and disaster risk.

9.3 Surface Water and Groundwater Systems

9.3.1 Surface Water

Includes rivers, lakes, and reservoirs.

These are visible sources but highly vulnerable to:

- Pollution
- Over-extraction
- Urban runoff
- Industrial discharge

9.3.2 Groundwater

Stored beneath Earth's surface in aquifers.

Groundwater:

- Supplies drinking water
- Supports irrigation
- Provides drought resilience

Over-extraction leads to:

- Aquifer depletion
- Land subsidence
- Saline intrusion in coastal areas

Groundwater recharge is often slower than withdrawal rates.

9.4 Water Scarcity: Physical and Economic Dimensions

Water scarcity manifests in two forms:

Physical Scarcity

- Insufficient natural water availability.

Economic Scarcity

- Adequate water exists, but infrastructure and governance limit access.
- Rapid urbanisation and population growth increase demand pressures.

Water stress can trigger:

- Agricultural loss
- Public health crises
- Migration
- Social conflict

Water security is therefore linked to national security.

9.5 Water and Climate Change

Climate change affects water systems by:

- Increasing rainfall variability
- Intensifying storms
- Expanding drought zones
- Accelerating glacier melt

Rising temperatures increase evaporation, reducing soil moisture.

Coastal flooding and sea-level rise threaten freshwater supplies through saltwater intrusion.

Adaptation planning must integrate water system resilience.

9.6 Agriculture and Water Use

Agriculture accounts for the largest share of freshwater withdrawals globally.

Inefficient irrigation systems contribute to water loss.

Sustainable practices include:

- Drip irrigation
- Rainwater harvesting
- Soil moisture monitoring
- Crop diversification

Water-efficient agriculture reduces vulnerability to climate shocks.

Food and water security are inseparable.

9.7 Urban Water Management

Urbanisation creates concentrated water demand.

Challenges include:

- Aging infrastructure
- Leakage
- Flood management
- Wastewater treatment capacity

Integrated urban water management promotes:

- Stormwater capture
- Green infrastructure
- Water recycling
- Smart metering systems

Cities must treat water as a cyclical resource, not a disposable commodity.

9.8 Industrial Water Use and Pollution

Industry requires water for:

- Cooling
- Processing
- Cleaning
- Energy production

Industrial discharge can introduce:

- Heavy metals
- Chemical contaminants
- Microplastics
- Thermal pollution

Strict effluent standards and monitoring systems are essential.

Polluted water increases treatment costs and health risks.

9.9 Wastewater Treatment and Circular Water Systems

Wastewater contains recoverable resources:

- Nutrients
- Energy (biogas)
- Reusable water

Advanced treatment systems enable:

- Water reuse for agriculture
- Industrial recycling
- Urban landscaping

Circular water systems reduce freshwater extraction and wastewater discharge.

Water reuse will become increasingly necessary in water-stressed regions.

9.10 Flood Risk and Disaster Management

Floods are among the costliest natural disasters.

Contributing factors include:

- Urban impermeable surfaces
- Deforestation
- River channel modification
- Climate-induced extreme rainfall

Nature-based flood solutions include:

- Wetland restoration
- River buffer zones
- Mangrove conservation

Disaster preparedness must integrate hydrological planning.

9.11 Water Governance and Institutional Coordination

Effective water governance requires:

- Clear regulatory frameworks
- Inter-agency coordination
- Data transparency
- Basin-level management

Fragmented governance leads to inefficiency.

Integrated Water Resources Management (IWRM) promotes coordinated development and management of water, land, and related resources.

Policy alignment reduces conflict between sectors.

9.12 Transboundary Water Cooperation

Many river basins cross national borders.

Shared water resources require:

- Cooperative agreements
- Conflict resolution mechanisms
- Shared data systems

Water diplomacy is increasingly important as climate variability intensifies.

Regional cooperation enhances stability.

9.13 Malaysia's Water Context

Malaysia receives high annual rainfall, yet faces periodic water stress due to:

- Uneven distribution
- Urban demand concentration
- Pollution
- Infrastructure limitations

Flooding during monsoon seasons coexists with drought conditions in certain regions.

National priorities include:

- Reducing non-revenue water (leakage losses)
- Improving wastewater treatment
- Strengthening watershed protection
- Enhancing flood mitigation infrastructure

Integrated planning is critical to long-term water security.

9.14 Water Pricing and Economic Signals

Water is often under-priced, leading to overconsumption.

Sustainable pricing frameworks must:

- Reflect treatment and infrastructure costs
- Protect vulnerable populations
- Encourage conservation

Tiered pricing structures incentivise efficient use.

However, water must remain accessible as a basic human necessity.

Balancing affordability and sustainability is central to policy design.

9.15 Water, Health and Social Stability

Unsafe water contributes to:

- Waterborne diseases
- Public health crises
- Economic productivity losses

Reliable access to clean water supports:

- Educational attendance
- Industrial productivity
- Healthcare resilience

Water infrastructure is social infrastructure.

9.16 Corporate Water Stewardship

Companies increasingly assess:

- Water footprint
- Basin-level risk exposure
- Supplier water practices

Water-intensive industries must implement:

- Efficiency improvements
- Recycling systems
- Pollution prevention

Water stewardship enhances ESG performance.

9.17 **Future Outlook: Climate-Resilient Water Systems**

Water governance must adapt to:

- Greater rainfall variability
- Higher temperatures
- Population growth
- Urban expansion

Resilient systems require:

- Infrastructure investment
- Ecosystem protection
- Digital monitoring
- Community engagement

Long-term planning reduces crisis management costs.

9.18 **Conclusion: Water as Strategic Resource**

Water connects:

- Climate systems
- Food production
- Biodiversity
- Public health
- Economic stability

Sustainability requires protecting both the quantity and quality of freshwater resources.

Water insecurity amplifies every other environmental risk.

In the next chapter, we examine sustainable cities and urban resilience understanding how urban systems can integrate energy, water, waste, biodiversity, and social equity into cohesive planning frameworks.

CHAPTER 10

SUSTAINABLE CITIES, URBAN RESILIENCE AND INFRASTRUCTURE PLANNING

10.1 Introduction: The Urban Century

The 21st century is the urban century.

More than half of the global population now lives in cities, and this proportion continues to rise. Cities generate:

- The majority of global GDP
- The majority of greenhouse gas emissions
- Significant resource consumption
- Concentrated waste production

Urban systems sit at the intersection of energy, water, transport, housing, and economic development.

If sustainability succeeds, it will succeed in cities. If it fails, urban instability will amplify global risk.

10.2 Cities as Metabolic Systems

Cities function as complex metabolic systems.

Inputs:

- Energy
- Water
- Food
- Raw materials

Outputs:

- Waste
- Emissions
- Wastewater
- Heat

Traditional urban planning followed a linear model: high throughput with limited recycling.

Sustainable urban systems must become circular, regenerative, and resilient.

Urban metabolism must align with ecological limits.

10.3 Urban Energy Systems

Cities are energy-intensive due to:

- Buildings
- Transport
- Industrial zones
- Commercial activity

Key strategies for decarbonising cities include:

- Renewable energy integration
- Rooftop solar deployment
- District cooling systems
- Smart grids
- Building retrofits

Buildings account for significant urban emissions. Energy-efficient design reduces long-term operating costs.

Urban energy planning is climate planning.

10.4 Sustainable Transport Systems

Urban mobility influences emissions, air quality, and social equity.

Sustainable transport prioritises:

- Public transit
- Electrified bus systems
- Rail infrastructure
- Cycling networks
- Pedestrian-friendly design

Car-dependent urban design increases congestion and emissions.

Transit-oriented development reduces sprawl and improves accessibility.

Mobility planning shapes environmental outcomes for decades.

10.5 Green Buildings and Low-Carbon Construction

Sustainable construction integrates:

- Energy efficiency
- Water efficiency
- Low-carbon materials
- Passive cooling design
- Natural lighting

Building certifications encourage improved performance standards.

Retrofitting existing building stock is as important as new construction.

Construction sector decarbonisation is central to climate mitigation.

10.6 Urban Heat Islands and Climate Adaptation

Urban heat islands occur when built surfaces absorb and retain heat.

Contributing factors include:

- Concrete surfaces
- Asphalt roads
- Limited vegetation
- High building density

Mitigation strategies include:

- Tree canopy expansion
- Reflective roofing materials
- Green roofs
- Urban parks

Heat mitigation protects public health and reduces energy demand.

10.7 Stormwater Management and Flood Resilience

Urban flooding results from:

- Impermeable surfaces
- Inadequate drainage
- Intense rainfall events

Sustainable drainage systems include:

- Rain gardens
- Permeable pavements
- Wetland restoration
- Retention basins

Nature-based solutions enhance resilience while improving biodiversity.

Flood-resilient design reduces economic disruption.

10.8 Waste Management in Urban Systems

Cities generate concentrated waste streams.

Effective urban waste systems integrate:

- Source separation
- Recycling infrastructure
- Composting facilities
- EPR compliance mechanisms
- Waste-to-energy (where appropriate)

Landfills near urban areas pose environmental and social risks.

Circular urban design reduces waste generation.

10.9 Affordable Housing and Social Sustainability

Urban sustainability is incomplete without social equity.

Housing affordability affects:

- Economic mobility
- Public health
- Community stability

Informal settlements often lack:

- Sanitation
- Clean water
- Waste collection
- Flood protection

Inclusive urban planning must address inequality.

Sustainability is environmental and social.

10.10 Digitalisation and Smart Cities

Smart technologies enable:

- Real-time traffic management
- Energy optimisation
- Water leakage detection
- Air quality monitoring

Digital tools improve resource efficiency and governance transparency.

However, technology must complement not replace structural sustainability planning.

Data enhances decision-making but does not substitute policy.

10.11 Urban Biodiversity Integration

Cities can integrate ecological systems through:

- Green corridors
- Urban forests
- Wetland buffers
- Community gardens

Urban biodiversity improves:

- Mental well-being
- Air quality
- Climate resilience

Nature must be embedded within urban landscapes.

10.12 Economic Clusters and Industrial Zones

Urban industrial zones influence emissions and pollution.

Sustainable industrial planning includes:

- Cleaner production standards
- Industrial symbiosis networks
- Waste heat recovery
- Emission monitoring

Eco-industrial parks reduce environmental footprint while maintaining competitiveness.

10.13 Governance and Multi-Level Coordination

Urban sustainability requires coordination across:

- Municipal authorities
- State governments
- National ministries
- Private developers
- Civil society

Fragmented governance undermines implementation.

Integrated urban planning frameworks enhance coherence.

10.14 Financing Urban Sustainability

Urban infrastructure requires substantial capital.

Financing tools include:

- Green municipal bonds
- Public-private partnerships
- Climate adaptation funds
- Sustainable development grants

Transparent procurement reduces corruption risk.

Long-term planning improves fiscal stability.

10.15 Malaysia's Urban Sustainability Landscape

Malaysia's major urban centres face:

- Rapid population growth
- Traffic congestion
- Flood vulnerability
- Waste management pressures

Strategic priorities include:

- Transit expansion
- Low-carbon development frameworks
- Flood mitigation investment
- Smart city integration
- Affordable housing initiatives

Urban resilience must align with national sustainability commitments.

10.16 Measuring Urban Sustainability

Indicators include:

- Air quality levels
- Public transport share
- Renewable energy penetration
- Waste diversion rates
- Green space per capita
- Flood incident frequency

Data-driven planning enhances accountability.

Benchmarking encourages continuous improvement.

10.17 Long-Term Urban Vision

Sustainable cities are:

- Low-carbon
- Climate-resilient
- Resource-efficient
- Inclusive
- Economically dynamic

Urban infrastructure decisions shape emissions and resource flows for decades.

Planning today determines resilience tomorrow.

10.18 Conclusion: Cities as Catalysts of Transformation

Cities concentrate both risk and opportunity.

They are:

- Major emitters
- Major innovators
- Economic engines
- Social laboratories

Sustainable urban transformation offers:

- Emission reductions
- Economic efficiency
- Improved quality of life
- Disaster resilience

In the next chapter, we examine sustainable consumption and behavioural change understanding how individual, corporate, and societal choices influence systemic outcomes.

CHAPTER 11

SUSTAINABLE CONSUMPTION, BEHAVIOURAL ECONOMICS AND LIFESTYLE TRANSITION

11.1 Introduction: Beyond Policy — The Human Factor

Sustainability is not achieved solely through regulation, infrastructure, or corporate reporting.

It is also shaped by:

- Individual choices
- Social norms
- Cultural values
- Consumer demand
- Behavioural incentives

Even the most well-designed sustainability policies can falter if behavioural systems remain unchanged.

Environmental transformation requires lifestyle transition.

11.2 The Consumption–Growth Paradigm

Modern economies have been structured around consumption-driven growth.

Characteristics include:

- Short product lifecycles
- Planned obsolescence

- Fast fashion
- Disposable packaging
- High resource throughput

Economic success has often been measured by increased consumption rather than improved well-being.

This paradigm places pressure on:

- Natural resources
- Waste systems
- Energy infrastructure

Rethinking consumption patterns is central to sustainable transition.

11.3 Ecological Footprint and Personal Impact

Every individual contributes to environmental impact through:

- Energy use
- Transportation
- Diet
- Purchasing habits
- Waste generation

The ecological footprint concept measures how much land and resources are required to sustain an individual's lifestyle.

While systemic change is essential, cumulative behavioural change significantly influences aggregate outcomes.

11.4 Behavioural Economics and Environmental Decision-Making

Traditional economic theory assumes rational decision-making.

Behavioural economics recognises that:

- People rely on habits
- Choices are influenced by framing
- Short-term rewards dominate long-term consequences
- Social norms shape behaviour

Environmental policy must account for cognitive biases.

Examples include:

- Default renewable energy options
- Visible recycling bins
- Deposit-return incentives
- Energy consumption feedback apps

Designing choice architecture influences outcomes without coercion.

11.5 Sustainable Consumption Principles

Sustainable consumption encourages:

1. Reduce – Limiting unnecessary purchases
2. Reuse – Extending product lifespans
3. Repair – Avoiding premature replacement
4. Recycle – Recovering materials responsibly
5. Rethink – Evaluating true necessity

Consumption should prioritise quality, durability, and functionality.

Value must shift from quantity to longevity.

11.6 Food Systems and Dietary Choices

Food production contributes significantly to:

- Greenhouse gas emissions
- Land use change
- Water consumption
- Biodiversity loss

Sustainable food practices include:

- Reducing food waste
- Diversifying protein sources
- Supporting sustainable agriculture
- Encouraging local sourcing where feasible

Dietary transitions can significantly reduce environmental footprint.

Food behaviour intersects with culture and identity.

Policy must respect social context.

11.7 Mobility and Lifestyle Emissions

Transportation choices influence emissions through:

- Private vehicle usage
- Public transport adoption
- Walking and cycling habits
- Air travel frequency

Urban design shapes mobility patterns.

Lifestyle transition toward low-carbon mobility requires:

- Infrastructure support
- Public trust in transit systems
- Behavioural incentives

Mobility decisions are influenced by convenience and accessibility.

11.8 Energy Use in Households

Households contribute to emissions through:

- Electricity consumption
- Cooling systems
- Appliances
- Lighting

Energy-efficient appliances and behavioural adjustments reduce consumption.

Smart meters and consumption feedback tools enhance awareness.

Behavioural change complements technological efficiency.

11.9 Waste Behaviour and Recycling Culture

Recycling success depends on:

- Clear labelling
- Accessible collection systems
- Public awareness
- Incentives

Confusion in waste sorting reduces recycling effectiveness.

Education and infrastructure must operate together.

Cultural norms strongly influence waste habits.

11.10 Consumer Power and Corporate Influence

Consumer demand influences corporate production patterns.

Purchasing decisions can encourage:

- Sustainable packaging
- Ethical sourcing
- Lower-carbon products

However, responsibility cannot rest solely on individuals.

Corporations shape available options.

Policy frameworks ensure that sustainable choices are accessible and affordable.

11.11 Social Norms and Peer Influence

People adjust behaviour based on perceived social norms.

Public campaigns highlighting collective participation increase adoption rates.

Examples include:

- Community recycling programs
- Public transport campaigns
- Energy-saving competitions

Collective identity strengthens behavioural adoption.

11.12 Education and Environmental Literacy

Environmental education supports:

- Scientific understanding
- Civic engagement
- Responsible consumption
- Long-term cultural change

Schools, universities, and public institutions play essential roles.

Education creates informed citizens capable of participating in sustainability governance.

11.13 Digital Platforms and Consumption Patterns

E-commerce and digital platforms influence:

- Purchasing frequency
- Packaging waste
- Delivery emissions

Digital transparency tools can:

- Provide carbon labels
- Offer sustainability comparisons
- Encourage responsible purchasing

Technology can either accelerate or reduce environmental impact.

Its effect depends on design and governance.

11.14 Equity and Sustainable Lifestyles

Not all consumers possess equal capacity to make sustainable choices.

Barriers include:

- Cost
- Accessibility
- Infrastructure gaps
- Information asymmetry

Policy must ensure that sustainable options are affordable and inclusive.

Lifestyle transition must not exacerbate inequality.

11.15 Policy Tools for Behavioural Change

Governments employ:

- Carbon pricing
- Plastic bag levies
- Deposit-return systems
- Energy efficiency standards
- Public awareness campaigns

Combining regulation with behavioural insights increases effectiveness.

Structural incentives accelerate cultural change.

11.16 Cultural Transformation and Long-Term Outlook

Sustainability requires cultural evolution:

- From disposability to durability
- From excess to sufficiency
- From ownership to shared access
- From short-termism to intergenerational thinking

Cultural shifts occur gradually but shape systemic transformation.

Values influence markets and policy alike.

11.17 Malaysia and Sustainable Consumption

Malaysia's sustainability transition includes:

- Plastic reduction initiatives
- Public recycling campaigns
- Sustainable food awareness programs

- Energy efficiency labelling
- ESG-driven corporate transparency

Urban youth engagement and educational initiatives play increasing roles.

Behavioural transition must align with national development goals.

11.18 Conclusion: Individual Action within Systemic Change

Individual choices alone cannot solve environmental crises.

However, they influence:

- Market demand
- Corporate strategy
- Political priorities
- Social norms

Sustainable consumption bridges:

- Policy
- Corporate governance
- Daily life

Systemic change requires both structural reform and behavioural participation.

In the next chapter, we expand toward governance architecture examining international environmental agreements, national policy alignment, and the future of global sustainability coordination.

CHAPTER 12

GLOBAL ENVIRONMENTAL GOVERNANCE AND INTERNATIONAL AGREEMENTS

12.1 Introduction: Environmental Problems Without Borders

Environmental challenges do not respect national boundaries.

- Carbon emissions disperse globally.
- Plastic pollution travels across oceans.
- River systems cross borders.
- Biodiversity loss affects planetary stability.

Because environmental risks are transboundary, governance must also operate beyond national jurisdictions.

Global environmental governance provides the framework for:

- Collective action
- Shared accountability
- Coordinated policy alignment

Without cooperation, national efforts risk being undermined by global inaction.

12.2 The Evolution of Global Environmental Governance

Modern international environmental governance began emerging in the late 20th century.

Early focus areas included:

- Ozone depletion
- Marine pollution
- Biodiversity protection

Over time, governance expanded to address:

- Climate change
- Desertification
- Sustainable development
- Plastic pollution

The global governance system evolved from isolated treaties to integrated sustainability frameworks.

12.3 Climate Agreements and Collective Responsibility

Global climate cooperation centers around multilateral agreements designed to limit greenhouse gas emissions.

The most significant framework today is the Paris Agreement.

The Paris Agreement established:

- A global temperature goal (well below 2°C, pursuing 1.5°C)
- Nationally Determined Contributions (NDCs)
- Five-year review cycles
- Transparency frameworks

Each country submits its own emissions reduction targets.

This bottom-up structure balances:

- National sovereignty
- Collective ambition

However, aggregate national pledges must align with scientific requirements to achieve temperature goals.

12.4 Sustainable Development as Integrated Policy

In 2015, the United Nations adopted the United Nations Sustainable Development Goals (SDGs).

The SDGs include 17 goals covering:

- Climate action
- Clean water
- Affordable energy
- Sustainable cities
- Responsible consumption
- Biodiversity protection
- Economic inclusion

The SDGs integrate environmental, social, and economic dimensions.

They reinforce the principle that sustainability is multidimensional.

12.5 Biodiversity Governance

Global biodiversity cooperation is structured around the Convention on Biological Diversity.

The Convention promotes:

- Conservation of biological diversity
- Sustainable use of its components
- Fair and equitable benefit-sharing

Recent global biodiversity frameworks aim to:

- Expand protected areas
- Reduce habitat destruction
- Restore degraded ecosystems

Biodiversity governance increasingly intersects with climate policy.

12.6 Ozone Protection as a Model of Success

One of the most successful international environmental agreements is the Montreal Protocol.

The Montreal Protocol phased out ozone-depleting substances.

Its success demonstrates that:

- Scientific consensus
- Regulatory clarity
- Industry adaptation
- International cooperation

can achieve measurable environmental recovery.

It serves as a model for climate and pollution agreements.

12.7 Plastic Pollution and Emerging Global Treaties

Plastic pollution has prompted negotiations toward a global plastics treaty.

Challenges include:

- Production caps
- Design standards
- Waste management infrastructure
- Transboundary waste trade

International cooperation is necessary to address marine plastic accumulation.

Waste exported across borders highlights governance gaps.

12.8 Financing Climate and Sustainability Transitions

Developing nations require financial support to:

- Transition energy systems
- Adapt to climate impacts
- Build resilience infrastructure

Climate finance mechanisms include:

- Green Climate Fund contributions
- Development bank financing
- Blended finance partnerships

Equitable financial distribution is central to global cooperation.

Without adequate support, developing countries face disproportionate burdens.

12.9 Common but Differentiated Responsibilities

International environmental law recognises the principle of:

Common but differentiated responsibilities (CBDR).

This principle acknowledges:

- All nations share responsibility for environmental protection.
- Developed nations historically contributed more to emissions.
- Developing nations require growth and poverty reduction.

CBDR seeks to balance environmental urgency with developmental equity.

12.10 Trade, Supply Chains and Environmental Standards

Global trade influences environmental outcomes through:

- Resource extraction
- Manufacturing emissions
- Waste flows

Trade policies increasingly incorporate:

- Environmental clauses
- Carbon border adjustments
- Sustainable sourcing requirements

Supply chain transparency supports global sustainability alignment.

12.11 Regional Cooperation in Southeast Asia

Regional platforms enhance coordination among neighbouring countries.

Key areas include:

- Transboundary haze pollution
- Marine resource management
- Disaster response coordination
- Renewable energy collaboration

Southeast Asia faces shared environmental risks requiring collective action.

Regional governance strengthens national efforts.

12.12 Enforcement Challenges

International environmental agreements face enforcement limitations.

Unlike domestic law, global treaties rely on:

- Diplomatic pressure
- Reporting transparency
- Peer accountability
- Reputational incentives

Non-compliance mechanisms are often limited.

Political will remains essential.

12.13 Climate Diplomacy and Geopolitical Dynamics

Climate negotiations intersect with:

- Energy security
- Trade competitiveness
- Geopolitical influence
- Technological leadership

Energy transition influences global power structures.

Countries investing in renewable technology gain strategic advantage.

Environmental diplomacy is increasingly central to foreign policy.

12.14 Integrating National Policy with Global Commitments

Countries must translate international agreements into domestic law.

This includes:

- Climate legislation
- EPR frameworks
- ESG reporting mandates
- Biodiversity conservation acts
- Renewable energy targets

National policy coherence determines implementation effectiveness.

Global commitments require local execution.

12.15 Malaysia in the Global Sustainability Landscape

Malaysia participates in:

- International climate agreements
- Biodiversity conventions
- Regional environmental cooperation

National strategies align with:

- Emissions reduction pathways
- Renewable energy expansion
- Circular economy frameworks
- Sustainable finance initiatives

International credibility strengthens economic competitiveness.

Alignment enhances investor confidence.

12.16 The Future of Global Environmental Governance

Emerging trends include:

- Mandatory climate disclosures
- Carbon border mechanisms
- Biodiversity financing frameworks
- Plastic production controls
- Nature-related financial risk assessments

Environmental governance is evolving from voluntary aspiration to structured accountability.

Institutional integration is accelerating.

12.17 Conclusion: Collective Action in an Interconnected World

Environmental sustainability cannot be achieved by isolated actors.

It requires:

- International cooperation
- National policy alignment
- Corporate accountability
- Citizen participation

Global environmental governance establishes the framework.

Domestic implementation determines impact.

In the next chapter, we examine implementation mechanisms at the national level exploring legislative frameworks, regulatory enforcement, and institutional coordination required to translate sustainability commitments into measurable outcomes.

CHAPTER 13

NATIONAL POLICY FRAMEWORKS, LEGISLATIVE INSTRUMENTS AND INSTITUTIONAL IMPLEMENTATION

13.1 Introduction: From Commitment to Execution

International agreements establish ambition. National frameworks determine implementation.

Sustainability becomes operational only when translated into:

- Legislation
- Regulatory standards
- Institutional mandates
- Enforcement mechanisms
- Budget allocations

Policy coherence, administrative capacity, and political commitment define outcomes.

Environmental transformation is ultimately a governance challenge.

13.2 The Architecture of Environmental Law

National sustainability frameworks typically consist of:

1. Framework Legislation
2. Sector-Specific Regulations
3. Administrative Guidelines

4. Enforcement Provisions
5. Judicial Oversight

Framework laws define overarching principles.

Sector regulations address:

- Air quality
- Water protection
- Waste management
- Climate mitigation
- Biodiversity conservation

Institutional coordination ensures policy alignment across ministries.

13.3 Environmental Impact Assessment (EIA)

Environmental Impact Assessment (EIA) is a preventive regulatory tool.

It requires developers to evaluate:

- Ecological impact
- Social implications
- Pollution risks
- Mitigation strategies

EIA promotes:

- Early-stage environmental integration
- Public consultation
- Evidence-based decision-making

Effective EIAs prevent long-term environmental costs.

Weak enforcement undermines credibility.

13.4 Climate Legislation and Carbon Governance

Climate governance at the national level includes:

- Emissions reduction targets
- Renewable energy mandates
- Energy efficiency standards
- Carbon pricing mechanisms
- Climate adaptation strategies

Legislative clarity provides:

- Investment certainty
- Policy stability
- Transparent accountability

Climate law increasingly intersects with financial regulation.

13.5 Waste Regulation and EPR Enforcement

National waste frameworks include:

- Recycling mandates
- Landfill standards
- Plastic bans
- Extended Producer Responsibility (EPR) systems
- Hazardous waste controls

EPR legislation requires:

- Producer registration
- Reporting obligations
- Fee structures
- Compliance verification

Enforcement integrity determines effectiveness.

13.6 Biodiversity and Land-Use Regulation

Land-use policies strongly influence biodiversity outcomes.

Key instruments include:

- Protected area designation
- Forest reserve classification
- Development zoning restrictions
- Wetland protection rules
- Wildlife conservation acts

Balancing development and conservation requires transparent planning processes.

Environmental permitting systems shape ecological preservation.

13.7 Institutional Coordination and Governance Complexity

Environmental governance involves multiple ministries:

- Environment
- Energy
- Finance
- Agriculture
- Transport
- Urban planning

Fragmentation can produce policy conflicts.

Examples include:

- Subsidising fossil fuels while promoting renewables
- Expanding agriculture into protected forests
- Encouraging industrial growth without pollution controls

Whole-of-government coordination enhances coherence.

13.8 Budgetary Alignment and Public Investment

Policy without funding is symbolic.

National budgets must allocate resources toward:

- Renewable infrastructure
- Flood mitigation systems
- Waste management facilities
- Environmental monitoring
- Enforcement personnel

Sustainable finance frameworks align public spending with climate goals.

Fiscal planning determines execution capacity.

13.9 Data Systems and Monitoring

Effective implementation requires:

- Reliable environmental data
- Emissions inventories
- Water quality monitoring
- Waste tracking systems
- Biodiversity indicators

Digital reporting platforms enhance transparency.

Accurate data enables policy adjustment.

Measurement precedes management.

13.10 Enforcement Mechanisms

Environmental law requires credible enforcement.

Tools include:

- Administrative fines
- License revocation
- Criminal penalties
- Civil liability
- Public disclosure requirements

Weak enforcement reduces deterrence.

Strong enforcement encourages compliance and fair competition.

13.11 Judicial and Public Participation

Courts play a critical role in:

- Reviewing environmental decisions
- Interpreting regulatory standards
- Protecting constitutional environmental rights (where applicable)

Public participation enhances accountability.

Community engagement improves legitimacy.

Transparency strengthens governance.

13.12 Policy Coherence Across Economic Planning

National development plans must align with:

- Climate commitments
- Biodiversity protection
- Circular economy goals
- ESG frameworks

Conflicting incentives undermine sustainability.

Integrated planning ensures that economic growth does not contradict environmental stability.

Long-term planning reduces policy reversals.

13.13 Role of Local Governments

Local authorities implement many sustainability measures, including:

- Waste collection
- Urban planning
- Water services
- Public transport
- Green space management

Capacity-building at municipal levels strengthens national outcomes.

Local innovation often drives practical solutions.

13.14 Private Sector Collaboration

Public-private partnerships accelerate infrastructure deployment.

Industry collaboration supports:

- Renewable energy expansion
- Recycling infrastructure
- Green technology development
- Sustainable agriculture programs

Regulatory clarity encourages private investment.

Cooperation enhances implementation speed.

13.15 Malaysia's Institutional Sustainability Framework

Malaysia's sustainability governance includes:

- Environmental quality legislation
- Renewable energy policies
- Green technology incentives
- EPR development frameworks
- Sustainable finance initiatives

Strategic priorities include:

- Carbon reduction commitments
- Flood resilience planning
- Plastic waste reduction
- Forest conservation

Inter-ministerial coordination remains essential for coherence.

13.16 Challenges in Implementation

Common barriers include:

- Regulatory overlap
- Capacity limitations
- Budget constraints
- Political transition
- Stakeholder resistance

Long-term stability enhances policy effectiveness.

Institutional continuity supports sustainable outcomes.

13.17 Transparency and Public Trust

Public confidence in sustainability governance depends on:

- Transparent reporting
- Clear targets
- Honest progress assessment
- Anti-corruption safeguards

Environmental governance intersects with good governance.

Trust strengthens compliance and citizen engagement.

13.18 Future Directions in National Sustainability Governance

Emerging trends include:

- Climate-related financial regulation
- Mandatory ESG disclosures
- Digital compliance platforms
- Carbon market development
- Nature-based solution integration

Policy evolution reflects growing environmental urgency.

National governance must adapt dynamically.

13.19 Conclusion: Governance as the Decisive Factor

Scientific understanding defines the problem.

Governance determines the response.

Sustainability requires:

- Clear legislation
- Institutional coordination

- Budgetary alignment
- Enforcement credibility
- Public participation

Policy architecture transforms aspiration into measurable progress.

In the next chapter, we examine sustainable finance, green investment frameworks, and the economic transformation required to fund long-term environmental resilience.

CHAPTER 14

SUSTAINABLE FINANCE, GREEN INVESTMENT AND ECONOMIC TRANSFORMATION

14.1 Introduction: Finance as a Climate Lever

Policy establishes direction. Technology enables transition. Finance determines scale and speed.

The transformation toward sustainability requires:

- Trillions in infrastructure investment
- Energy system redesign
- Industrial decarbonisation
- Biodiversity protection
- Climate adaptation infrastructure

Capital allocation determines whether sustainability remains theoretical or becomes structural.

Financial systems are therefore central to environmental transition.

14.2 From Traditional Finance to Sustainable Finance

Traditional finance evaluates:

- Profitability
- Risk
- Return on investment
- Market performance

Sustainable finance expands this lens to include:

- Environmental risk
- Social impact
- Governance integrity
- Long-term resilience

Financial systems are increasingly integrating non-financial risk factors.

Climate risk is now recognised as financial risk.

14.3 The Rise of ESG Integration

Environmental, Social and Governance (ESG) criteria have become central to modern investment analysis.

Environmental factors include:

- Carbon emissions
- Resource efficiency
- Waste management
- Biodiversity impact

Social factors include:

- Labour practices
- Community relations
- Human rights

Governance factors include:

- Board accountability
- Transparency
- Anti-corruption measures

ESG integration shifts capital toward companies aligned with sustainability.

14.4 Climate Risk and Financial Stability

Climate risk manifests in two primary forms:

1. Physical Risk
    - Floods
    - Heatwaves
    - Storm damage
    - Agricultural disruption
2. Transition Risk
    - Carbon regulation
    - Technological disruption
    - Stranded fossil assets
    - Changing consumer preferences

Financial regulators increasingly require climate risk disclosure to maintain systemic stability.

Unmanaged climate risk threatens banking and insurance sectors.

14.5 Green Bonds and Sustainable Financing Instruments

Green financial instruments include:

- Green bonds
- Sustainability-linked loans
- Climate bonds
- Transition bonds
- Social bonds

Green bonds finance projects such as:

- Renewable energy
- Energy-efficient buildings

- Clean transport
- Waste management systems
- Flood mitigation infrastructure

Transparent reporting enhances investor confidence.

14.6 Carbon Markets and Pricing Mechanisms

Carbon pricing instruments include:

- Carbon taxes
- Emissions trading systems
- Voluntary carbon markets

Carbon markets create economic incentives for emission reduction.

However, effectiveness depends on:

- Price integrity
- Verification standards
- Avoidance of double counting
- Transparent governance

Carbon pricing internalises environmental externalities.

14.7 Sustainable Banking and Regulatory Supervision

Central banks and financial regulators are increasingly incorporating sustainability into supervisory frameworks.

Emerging practices include:

- Climate stress testing
- Sustainable lending taxonomies
- Green asset classification systems
- Mandatory sustainability disclosures

Financial institutions are transitioning from voluntary ESG to regulated sustainability reporting.

14.8 Corporate Disclosure and Reporting Standards

Sustainability disclosure frameworks enhance comparability and transparency.

Global reporting systems aim to standardise:

- Emissions accounting
- Supply chain risk
- Biodiversity exposure
- Climate adaptation strategies

Consistent disclosure reduces greenwashing.

Investors increasingly demand credible, verifiable data.

14.9 Transition Finance for Emerging Economies

Developing countries require:

- Infrastructure financing
- Renewable energy capital
- Adaptation funding
- Resilience investment

Blended finance models combine:

- Public capital
- Multilateral support
- Private sector investment

Transition finance recognises that decarbonisation pathways vary across economies.

Equitable capital distribution is essential.

14.10 The Role of Development Banks

Multilateral development banks support:

- Climate adaptation
- Renewable expansion
- Water infrastructure
- Disaster resilience

Public finance often catalyses private investment.

Strategic public funding reduces perceived investment risk.

14.11 Sustainable Taxonomies and Classification Systems

Sustainable taxonomies define what qualifies as "green."

Clear classification prevents:

- Mislabelled investments
- Greenwashing
- Regulatory confusion

Taxonomies typically include:

- Emissions thresholds
- Environmental performance criteria
- Sector-specific benchmarks

Standardisation improves cross-border capital flows.

14.12 Biodiversity Finance and Nature-Based Investment

Financial systems are expanding beyond carbon to nature protection.

Nature-based solutions include:

- Forest restoration
- Mangrove rehabilitation

- Watershed protection
- Coastal resilience infrastructure

Biodiversity loss presents material financial risk.

Capital markets increasingly recognise ecosystem services as economic assets.

14.13 Economic Diversification and Industrial Transformation

Sustainability requires structural economic shifts:

- From fossil fuel dependency
- Toward renewable and green industries
- From extractive models
- Toward regenerative economic systems

Industrial policy plays a key role in:

- Green manufacturing
- Battery production
- Sustainable agriculture
- Circular economy infrastructure

Economic diversification strengthens resilience.

14.14 Malaysia's Sustainable Finance Landscape

Malaysia has advanced sustainability finance through:

- Green sukuk frameworks
- Sustainable investment guidelines
- Renewable energy financing mechanisms
- ESG reporting initiatives

Financial institutions increasingly integrate climate risk assessments.

Capital markets are aligning with:

- Net-zero commitments
- Circular economy development
- ESG disclosure requirements

Malaysia's regional positioning strengthens its sustainable finance ecosystem.

14.15 Challenges in Sustainable Finance

Key challenges include:

- Inconsistent global standards
- Greenwashing risks
- Limited high-quality project pipelines
- Data reliability concerns
- Short-term investment horizons

Financial transformation requires regulatory clarity and institutional trust.

Long-term alignment is essential.

14.16 Aligning Profit with Planet

Sustainable finance reframes value creation.

Long-term profitability increasingly depends on:

- Resource efficiency
- Climate resilience
- Regulatory compliance
- Stakeholder trust

Sustainability and profitability are no longer mutually exclusive.

Risk-adjusted returns increasingly favour responsible investment.

14.17 The Future of Sustainable Capital Markets

Emerging trends include:

- Mandatory climate disclosures
- Carbon accounting integration
- Transition finance frameworks
- Nature-related financial risk reporting
- ESG-linked executive compensation

Financial systems are shifting from optional sustainability to embedded accountability.

Capital will increasingly flow toward sustainable assets.

14.18 Conclusion: Financing the Transition

Environmental ambition requires economic backing.

Sustainable finance provides:

- Incentive alignment
- Risk management
- Capital mobilisation
- Accountability structures

The global transition depends not only on policy and technology, but on where money flows.

Capital allocation shapes the future.

CHAPTER 15

INNOVATION, TECHNOLOGY AND THE FUTURE OF SUSTAINABLE DEVELOPMENT

15.1 Introduction: Innovation as a Catalyst

Throughout history, technological innovation has reshaped civilisation.

Today, innovation must address a different imperative:

- Decarbonisation
- Resource efficiency
- Ecological restoration
- Climate adaptation
- Circular production systems

Technology alone cannot solve environmental challenges.

However, without innovation, sustainability transition cannot occur at the required scale or speed.

15.2 Clean Energy Transformation

Energy systems sit at the centre of climate transition.

Technological advancement in:

- Solar photovoltaics
- Wind energy systems
- Hydropower optimisation

- Battery storage
- Grid digitalisation

has reduced costs and expanded deployment.

Renewable energy competitiveness is accelerating global energy transformation.

Grid modernisation ensures reliability and flexibility.

15.3 Energy Storage and Battery Innovation

Energy storage addresses intermittency challenges in renewable systems.

Battery technology innovation focuses on:

- Increased energy density
- Reduced material intensity
- Recycling capability
- Cost reduction

Research into alternative battery chemistries aims to reduce dependence on scarce minerals.

Storage solutions extend beyond batteries to include:

- Pumped hydro
- Thermal storage
- Hydrogen systems

15.4 Hydrogen and Industrial Decarbonisation

Green hydrogen offers potential for:

- Heavy industry decarbonisation
- Shipping
- Aviation
- Chemical production

Hydrogen's role depends on:

- Renewable energy availability
- Infrastructure investment
- Cost competitiveness

Hard-to-abate sectors require technological breakthroughs.

15.5 Carbon Capture and Utilisation

Carbon capture technologies aim to:

- Remove emissions from industrial processes
- Capture atmospheric carbon
- Convert CO_2 into usable products

Debate surrounds:

- Cost-effectiveness
- Long-term storage security
- Risk of prolonging fossil fuel use

Carbon removal may complement emission reduction but cannot replace it.

15.6 Digital Technology and Environmental Monitoring

Digital innovation enhances sustainability through:

- Satellite monitoring of deforestation
- AI-based energy optimisation
- Smart grids
- Precision agriculture
- Waste tracking platforms

Data analytics improves resource efficiency.

Transparency strengthens accountability.

15.7 Artificial Intelligence and Sustainability

Artificial intelligence (AI) contributes to:

- Climate modelling
- Disaster prediction
- Supply chain optimisation
- Energy demand forecasting
- Environmental risk assessment

However, AI systems also consume energy.

Sustainable AI design requires:

- Energy-efficient computing
- Renewable-powered data centres
- Responsible deployment

Technology must be managed responsibly.

15.8 Circular Design and Materials Innovation

Product design influences environmental impact.

Innovation in materials includes:

- Biodegradable polymers
- Recycled composites
- Modular product architecture
- Low-carbon cement alternatives

Circular design reduces lifecycle emissions.

Durability and reparability support resource conservation.

15.9 Sustainable Agriculture and Food Technology

Technological advancements in agriculture include:

- Precision irrigation
- Climate-resilient crops
- Alternative proteins
- Vertical farming
- Soil carbon measurement tools

Agricultural innovation must balance:

- Productivity
- Biodiversity protection
- Water conservation

Food security and sustainability are interconnected.

15.10 Urban Innovation and Smart Cities

Urban areas concentrate population and emissions.

Smart city technologies improve:

- Traffic flow
- Public transport efficiency
- Energy use in buildings
- Waste management
- Water distribution systems

Integrated planning enhances environmental performance.

Urban innovation supports climate resilience.

15.11 Nature-Based Solutions and Ecological Engineering

Innovation is not limited to digital systems.

Nature-based solutions include:

- Mangrove restoration
- Reforestation
- Wetland rehabilitation
- Green urban infrastructure

Ecological engineering integrates natural systems into resilience planning.

These approaches often provide cost-effective adaptation.

15.12 Industrial Transformation and Green Manufacturing

Industrial innovation focuses on:

- Electrification of processes
- Low-carbon steel production
- Sustainable cement alternatives
- Circular material flows

Manufacturing redesign reduces resource intensity.

Green industrial policy supports technological transition.

15.13 Financing Innovation

Innovation requires:

- Research and development funding
- Venture capital
- Public-private partnerships
- Government grants
- Innovation ecosystems

Early-stage technologies often face:

- High risk
- Limited commercial viability
- Scaling challenges

Strategic investment accelerates adoption.

15.14 Ethical and Governance Considerations

Technological innovation must consider:

- Social equity
- Labour transitions
- Digital privacy
- Environmental justice

Green technology should not create new inequalities.

Responsible governance ensures inclusive benefits.

15.15 Malaysia's Innovation Landscape

Malaysia is expanding:

- Renewable energy deployment
- Green technology incentives
- Circular economy innovation
- Sustainable finance instruments
- Climate resilience planning

Technology hubs and universities support research and development.

Public policy alignment encourages innovation adoption.

Regional positioning enhances collaboration opportunities.

15.16 Innovation Barriers

Common obstacles include:

- High capital cost
- Infrastructure limitations
- Regulatory uncertainty
- Technology acceptance
- Skills shortages

Policy stability enhances investor confidence.

Education and workforce development support technological transition.

15.17 Future Horizons

Emerging areas include:

- Direct air carbon capture
- Advanced battery recycling
- Sustainable aviation fuels
- Nature-positive finance models
- AI-driven climate governance

The pace of innovation is accelerating.

Technological progress must align with ecological limits.

15.18 Conclusion: Technology within Governance

Innovation expands possibility.

Governance defines direction.

Sustainability requires:

- Scientific research
- Responsible deployment

- Regulatory clarity
- Public acceptance
- Ethical safeguards

Technology accelerates transition but must operate within environmental boundaries.

In the next chapter, we conclude the manuscript by synthesising governance, finance, innovation, and behavioural transformation into a unified sustainability pathway.

CHAPTER 16

TOWARD AN INTEGRATED SUSTAINABILITY FUTURE: POLICY, CAPITAL, TECHNOLOGY AND CULTURE

16.1 Introduction: The Convergence Imperative

Sustainability is not a single-discipline challenge.

It is not solely:

- An environmental issue
- An economic reform
- A governance adjustment
- A technological problem
- A behavioural shift

It is all of these simultaneously.

The defining task of the 21st century is integration.

Fragmented solutions will not produce systemic transformation.

16.2 The Four Pillars of Sustainable Transformation

This book has examined sustainability through four structural pillars:

1. Policy and Governance
2. Finance and Capital Allocation
3. Innovation and Technology
4. Behavioural and Cultural Transition

Individually, each pillar influences change. Collectively, they enable transformation.

The absence of any one pillar weakens the whole system.

16.3 Policy: Setting Direction and Guardrails

Governance defines:

- Targets
- Standards
- Accountability
- Enforcement
- Incentives

Policy aligns national frameworks with international commitments such as the Paris Agreement.

It embeds sustainability into:

- Legislation
- Budget planning
- Institutional coordination
- Regulatory supervision

Without policy clarity, markets lack certainty.

16.4 Finance: Mobilising Capital at Scale

Capital allocation determines infrastructure transformation.

Sustainable finance directs investment toward:

- Renewable energy
- Circular manufacturing
- Biodiversity protection
- Climate resilience

ESG frameworks, green bonds, and carbon pricing mechanisms reshape risk perception.

When finance integrates environmental risk, long-term stability improves.

16.5 Technology: Accelerating Practical Solutions

Innovation enables:

- Clean energy deployment
- Industrial decarbonisation
- Resource efficiency
- Climate monitoring
- Smart infrastructure

Technology lowers cost barriers and improves scalability.

However, technology must operate within regulatory and ethical boundaries.

Innovation without governance risks unintended consequences.

16.6 Culture: The Invisible Infrastructure

Cultural values influence:

- Consumption patterns
- Corporate behaviour
- Political priorities
- Social norms

Sustainability requires a cultural shift:

- From excess to sufficiency
- From disposability to durability
- From short-term profit to long-term resilience

Policy and finance may incentivise change, but culture sustains it.

16.7 Interdependency of Systems

The four pillars are interconnected.

Policy influences finance. Finance supports innovation. Innovation shapes consumption. Culture influences political mandate.

Systemic change requires feedback loops that reinforce sustainability objectives.

Disjointed implementation reduces effectiveness.

16.8 Climate Resilience and Adaptation

Even with mitigation efforts, climate impacts are unavoidable.

Adaptation requires:

- Flood mitigation infrastructure
- Coastal protection
- Water management systems
- Heat-resilient urban design
- Agricultural diversification

Resilience must be embedded into national planning.

Prevention reduces long-term economic loss.

16.9 Biodiversity and Ecological Stability

Climate policy alone is insufficient.

Ecosystem degradation threatens:

- Food security
- Water systems
- Carbon sinks
- Public health

Integrated sustainability includes:

- Forest conservation
- Marine protection
- Wetland restoration
- Sustainable land-use planning

Nature underpins economic stability.

16.10 Circular Economy as Structural Redesign

Circular economy models reduce:

- Resource extraction
- Waste generation
- Emissions intensity

They require:

- EPR enforcement
- Product redesign
- Recycling infrastructure
- Market incentives

Circularity integrates industrial policy with behavioural change.

16.11 Youth, Education and Intergenerational Responsibility

Young generations inherit long-term consequences.

Education systems must prepare future leaders to:

- Understand ecological limits
- Integrate sustainability into business
- Engage in policy design
- Drive innovation responsibly

Intergenerational equity is central to sustainability governance.

16.12 Private Sector Leadership

Corporate actors shape:

- Supply chains
- Investment flows
- Production patterns
- Consumer access

Responsible leadership includes:

- Transparent ESG reporting
- Science-based climate targets
- Ethical governance
- Sustainable product design

Private sector alignment accelerates systemic transition.

16.13 Malaysia's Integrated Pathway

Malaysia's sustainability trajectory includes:

- Renewable energy expansion
- Sustainable finance growth
- ESG regulatory development
- Circular economy initiatives
- Biodiversity conservation efforts

National competitiveness increasingly depends on sustainability credibility.

Regional leadership enhances economic resilience.

Integrated implementation strengthens global positioning.

16.14 Global Cooperation in a Fragmented World

Geopolitical complexity challenges cooperation.

Yet environmental interdependence makes collaboration unavoidable.

Global agreements, technology transfer, and climate finance remain essential.

Shared risk requires shared responsibility.

Multilateral engagement strengthens stability.

16.15 The Cost of Inaction

Failure to act produces:

- Economic disruption
- Supply chain instability
- Insurance system strain
- Public health crises
- Social inequality

Environmental degradation carries financial consequences.

Delayed action increases cumulative cost.

Prevention is more efficient than recovery.

16.16 Measuring Progress

Sustainability progress must be measurable.

Indicators include:

- Emissions trajectories
- Renewable energy penetration
- Waste recovery rates

- Biodiversity restoration
- ESG compliance

Transparent measurement builds accountability.

Data integrity supports policy refinement.

16.17 A Strategic Roadmap Forward

An integrated sustainability strategy requires:

1. Legislative clarity
2. Capital mobilisation
3. Technological innovation
4. Cultural engagement
5. Institutional coordination
6. International alignment

Each dimension reinforces the others.

Fragmented progress must evolve into systemic integration.

16.18 Conclusion: A Shared Responsibility

Sustainability is not a temporary policy trend.

It is a structural transformation of:

- Economic systems
- Governance architecture
- Financial markets
- Technological design
- Social values

The transition demands:

- Leadership
- Evidence-based policy
- Ethical governance
- Collective participation

The future of sustainable development depends on alignment.

Policy must be ambitious. Capital must be responsible. Technology must be ethical. Culture must be conscious.

Together, they define the path forward.

PART III

WASTE, RESOURCES AND CIRCULAR ECONOMY

CHAPTER 17

FROM LINEAR EXTRACTION TO CIRCULAR REGENERATION

17.1 The Structural Problem of Linear Growth

Modern industrial systems developed under a linear economic paradigm:

Extract → Produce → Consume → Dispose

This model assumes:

- Infinite resource availability
- Unlimited ecological absorption capacity
- Externalised environmental costs

The linear economy accelerated industrialisation and global trade, but it also produced:

- Resource depletion
- Waste accumulation
- Marine plastic pollution
- Landfill saturation
- Greenhouse gas emissions

The environmental crisis is therefore not accidental it is systemic.

17.2 Resource Scarcity and Economic Vulnerability

Natural resources underpin industrial production. However:

- Critical minerals are geopolitically concentrated
- Fossil fuels drive carbon dependency
- Land degradation threatens food systems
- Water scarcity affects industrial productivity

Resource insecurity increases economic volatility.

Sustainable governance must treat resource efficiency as economic policy not merely environmental protection.

17.3 Waste as a Governance Failure

Waste represents:

- Inefficient design
- Market failure
- Regulatory gaps
- Behavioural misalignment

Landfill disposal transfers environmental cost to future generations.

Waste mismanagement also contributes to methane emissions a potent greenhouse gas.

Poorly regulated waste streams can undermine public health and ecological integrity.

17.4 The Conceptual Foundation of the Circular Economy

The circular economy seeks to redesign production systems so that:

- Materials remain in use
- Waste is eliminated by design
- Products are repairable and reusable
- Biological materials regenerate ecosystems

It challenges the assumption that economic growth requires resource depletion.

17.5 Linear vs Circular Economy

Linear Model:

- Raw material extraction
- Manufacturing
- Consumption
- Disposal

Circular Model:

- Sustainable sourcing
- Eco-design
- Reuse
- Repair
- Refurbishment
- Recycling
- Regeneration

Circular systems reduce extraction intensity and environmental degradation.

CHAPTER 18

WASTE HIERARCHY AND RESOURCE EFFICIENCY

18.1 The Waste Hierarchy Framework

The waste hierarchy establishes priority order:

1. Prevention
2. Reduction
3. Reuse
4. Recycling
5. Recovery
6. Disposal

Disposal is the least desirable outcome.

The hierarchy shifts policy from end-of-pipe solutions to upstream design reform.

18.2 Prevention as Primary Strategy

The most effective waste policy is waste avoidance.

This requires:

- Sustainable product design
- Minimal packaging
- Extended product lifespan
- Demand-side efficiency

Prevention reduces system-wide cost.

18.3 Recycling and Its Structural Limits

Recycling remains important but:

- It requires energy
- Material quality may degrade
- Infrastructure investment is high
- Market prices fluctuate

Overreliance on recycling without redesign perpetuates inefficiency.

Circular economy prioritises redesign over recycling.

18.4 Landfill and Environmental Externalities

Landfills generate:

- Methane emissions
- Soil contamination
- Leachate pollution
- Long-term land use restrictions

Methane emissions from landfills contribute to climate change.

Reducing landfill dependency is both environmental and economic policy.

CHAPTER 19

EXTENDED PRODUCER RESPONSIBILITY (EPR)

19.1 Regulatory Rationale

Extended Producer Responsibility shifts waste management responsibility from municipalities to producers.

The principle aligns with:

- Polluter Pays Principle
- Environmental accountability
- Market internalisation of waste costs

EPR incentivises producers to:

- Design recyclable products
- Reduce packaging
- Improve material efficiency

19.2 Comparative Regulatory Models

EPR schemes exist across multiple jurisdictions, including the European Union.

The EU Waste Framework Directive mandates producer responsibility systems.

EPR structures vary:

- Collective compliance schemes
- Individual producer responsibility
- Deposit-return systems

Regulatory clarity determines effectiveness.

19.3 EPR and Plastic Waste

Plastic pollution requires systemic intervention.

EPR for packaging encourages:

- Recyclable material use
- Reduction in single-use plastics
- Financing of recycling infrastructure

Without regulatory enforcement, voluntary compliance is insufficient.

19.4 Malaysian Context

Malaysia faces:

- High plastic consumption
- Growing urban waste
- Recycling rate improvement challenges

EPR implementation could:

- Reduce landfill pressure
- Improve material recovery
- Encourage domestic recycling industry growth

Policy integration with national sustainability targets is essential.

CHAPTER 20

INDUSTRIAL REDESIGN AND CIRCULAR BUSINESS MODELS

20.1 Product-as-a-Service Models

Instead of selling products, companies provide services.

Example:

- Leasing rather than selling equipment

This incentivises durability and repairability.

20.2 Design for Disassembly

Products should be:

- Modular
- Easy to repair
- Easy to upgrade
- Material-identifiable

Design reform reduces downstream waste.

20.3 Industrial Symbiosis

Industrial by-products from one sector become inputs for another.

This reduces:

- Raw material demand
- Waste disposal
- Production cost

Symbiotic systems enhance industrial efficiency.

CHAPTER 21

CARBON CYCLE AND RESOURCE SYSTEMS

21.1 The Natural Carbon Cycle

The carbon cycle includes:

- Atmospheric carbon dioxide
- Ocean absorption
- Photosynthesis
- Soil carbon storage

Human activity disrupts this equilibrium.

21.2 Waste and Methane Emissions

Organic waste decomposition produces methane.

Methane has a significantly higher short-term warming potential than carbon dioxide.

Reducing organic landfill disposal mitigates emissions.

21.3 Circularity and Climate Mitigation

Circular economy reduces emissions by:

- Reducing extraction
- Lowering production energy
- Extending product lifespan
- Improving material efficiency

Circularity is therefore climate policy.

CHAPTER 22

GOVERNANCE ARCHITECTURE FOR CIRCULAR TRANSITION

22.1 Policy Integration

Circular transition requires coordination across:

- Environmental law
- Industrial policy
- Trade regulation
- Financial incentives

Fragmented policy reduces impact.

22.2 Sustainable Finance and Circular Investment

Green financing mechanisms support:

- Recycling plants
- Waste-to-energy facilities
- Circular startups
- Eco-design innovation

Capital allocation determines transition speed.

22.3 Enforcement and Compliance

Effective circular governance requires:

- Data transparency
- Reporting standards
- Regulatory supervision
- Penalties for non-compliance

Weak enforcement undermines reform.

22.4 Public Awareness and Cultural Change

Behavioural patterns influence waste generation.

Education promotes:

- Responsible consumption
- Waste segregation
- Product care
- Community recycling participation

Cultural transition supports policy implementation.

CHAPTER 23

FUTURE OUTLOOK: CIRCULAR ECONOMY AS ECONOMIC STRATEGY

23.1 Competitiveness and Innovation

Countries leading circular innovation gain:

- Export advantages
- Technology leadership
- ESG investment flows

Circular economy enhances economic resilience.

23.2 Digital Technology and Resource Tracking

Blockchain and AI systems can:

- Track material flows
- Improve supply chain transparency
- Enhance recycling efficiency

Digital governance strengthens accountability.

23.3 Regional Leadership Opportunities

Malaysia and ASEAN can:

- Develop harmonised EPR standards
- Build regional recycling markets
- Attract sustainable finance

Strategic positioning enhances competitiveness.

Concluding Reflection

Waste is not merely discarded material.

It is a design signal.

Circular economy reform is not environmental idealism it is industrial restructuring.

The transition from linear extraction to regenerative systems defines the next phase of economic evolution.

PART IV

EXTENDED PRODUCER RESPONSIBILITY AND POLICY INSTRUMENTS

CHAPTER 24

THE LEGAL FOUNDATIONS OF EXTENDED PRODUCER RESPONSIBILITY

24.1 Introduction: From Waste Management to Producer Accountability

Waste governance has historically been municipal.

Local authorities collected, transported, and disposed of waste using public funds. This model created structural distortions:

- Producers externalised disposal costs
- Consumers lacked disposal incentives
- Governments bore financial burden
- Landfills expanded

Extended Producer Responsibility (EPR) restructured this paradigm by shifting financial and operational responsibility upstream to producers.

EPR aligns environmental cost with product origin.

24.2 Normative Foundations

EPR is grounded in three principles:

1. Polluter Pays Principle
2. Lifecycle Responsibility
3. Internalisation of Externalities

The Polluter Pays Principle is embedded in numerous international environmental frameworks and national environmental statutes.

EPR operationalises this principle in product systems.

24.3 International Legal Anchors

Global environmental governance has reinforced producer accountability through instruments such as:

- Basel Convention
- Stockholm Convention
- Organisation for Economic Co-operation and Development EPR guidelines

The OECD has been particularly influential in conceptualising and standardising EPR frameworks.

CHAPTER 25

COMPARATIVE EPR MODELS

25.1 European Union Model

The European Union has advanced one of the most comprehensive EPR systems globally under the Waste Framework Directive.

Member States implement:

- Packaging EPR
- Electrical and Electronic Equipment (WEEE) schemes
- Battery directives
- End-of-life vehicle regulations

EPR in the EU integrates reporting, compliance schemes, and recycling targets.

25.2 Deposit Return Systems

Deposit return systems (DRS) operate on refundable consumer deposits.

These systems have demonstrated high recovery rates for beverage containers.

They create:

- Consumer financial incentive
- Reduced litter
- High-quality recycling streams

25.3 Individual vs Collective Compliance

Two major compliance structures exist:

Collective Systems

- Producers join a compliance organisation
- Shared financial and operational responsibility

Individual Responsibility

- Producers manage their own recovery systems

Regulatory oversight determines transparency and performance.

CHAPTER 26

EPR AND PLASTIC GOVERNANCE

26.1 Plastic as a Structural Challenge

Plastic waste has become one of the most visible environmental crises.

Characteristics:

- Durability
- Low degradation
- High consumption rate
- Marine leakage

EPR addresses plastic waste through:

- Packaging levies
- Mandatory recycling content
- Producer reporting obligations

26.2 Global Plastic Negotiations

Ongoing international negotiations aim to establish a global plastic treaty under the United Nations framework.

This initiative reflects recognition that plastic pollution transcends national boundaries.

26.3 Financing Recycling Infrastructure

EPR funds support:

- Material recovery facilities
- Waste sorting systems
- Collection logistics
- Public awareness campaigns

Financial sustainability is central to long-term effectiveness.

CHAPTER 27

ECONOMIC INSTRUMENTS IN ENVIRONMENTAL POLICY

EPR operates within broader environmental policy instruments.

27.1 Market-Based Mechanisms

Market-based instruments include:

- Carbon pricing
- Environmental taxes
- Subsidies for green technology
- Tradable permits

Carbon pricing mechanisms are often aligned with climate commitments under the Paris Agreement.

27.2 Regulatory Instruments

Command-and-control regulation includes:

- Emission limits
- Recycling targets
- Product standards
- Mandatory disclosures

While less flexible than market instruments, they ensure minimum compliance.

27.3 Hybrid Policy Design

Effective sustainability governance often combines:

- Regulatory standards
- Financial incentives
- Reporting obligations
- Public-private partnerships

Hybrid systems balance flexibility and enforceability.

CHAPTER 28

ESG AND CORPORATE ACCOUNTABILITY

28.1 ESG as Complementary Framework

Environmental, Social and Governance (ESG) reporting complements EPR by:

- Increasing transparency
- Aligning investor expectations
- Enhancing corporate accountability

ESG shifts sustainability from compliance obligation to strategic imperative.

28.2 Global ESG Standardisation

International standard-setting bodies such as the International Sustainability Standards Board have developed disclosure frameworks.

Standardisation improves comparability across markets.

28.3 Investor Pressure and Capital Allocation

Institutional investors increasingly integrate ESG metrics into portfolio decisions.

Capital markets thus reinforce regulatory objectives.

CHAPTER 29

MALAYSIA'S POLICY LANDSCAPE

29.1 Waste Governance Structure

Malaysia's waste governance involves federal and state coordination.

Challenges include:

- Infrastructure gaps
- Public awareness
- Informal sector integration

29.2 EPR Development

Malaysia has begun policy discussions regarding EPR for packaging waste.

Successful implementation requires:

- Legislative clarity
- Industry consultation
- Phased implementation
- Data reporting systems

29.3 Regional Alignment

ASEAN cooperation could enhance:

- Harmonised standards
- Shared recycling markets
- Cross-border waste regulation

Regional collaboration strengthens competitiveness.

CHAPTER 30

ENFORCEMENT, COMPLIANCE AND ACCOUNTABILITY

30.1 Monitoring Systems

EPR effectiveness depends on:

- Accurate reporting
- Independent audits
- Transparent compliance registers

Data integrity is foundational.

30.2 Penalties and Incentives

Regulatory frameworks must balance:

- Financial penalties
- Market incentives
- Compliance rewards

Weak enforcement undermines credibility.

30.3 Institutional Capacity

Regulatory agencies require:

- Technical expertise
- Digital monitoring systems
- Inter-agency coordination

Capacity-building is a structural necessity.

CHAPTER 31

THE FUTURE OF PRODUCER RESPONSIBILITY

31.1 Digital Tracking and Traceability

Emerging technologies enable:

- Blockchain-based material tracking
- AI-assisted waste analytics
- Smart labelling systems

Digitalisation enhances transparency.

31.2 Circular Economy Integration

EPR should evolve beyond waste management into:

- Product redesign
- Circular supply chain integration
- Sustainable procurement standards

Producer responsibility becomes industrial policy.

31.3 Global Harmonisation

Fragmented regulatory regimes increase compliance costs.

Harmonised frameworks support:

- Trade stability
- Investment certainty
- Environmental consistency

International coordination remains critical.

Concluding Reflection

Extended Producer Responsibility is not merely a waste policy instrument.

It is:

- A governance reform
- A market correction mechanism
- A corporate accountability tool
- A circular economy enabler

When combined with financial instruments, ESG disclosure, and regulatory enforcement, EPR becomes a central pillar of sustainability transformation.

PART V

ESG, CORPORATE SUSTAINABILITY & FINANCE

CHAPTER 32

THE EVOLUTION OF ESG: FROM VOLUNTARY ETHICS TO REGULATORY ARCHITECTURE

32.1 Introduction

Environmental, Social and Governance (ESG) frameworks have transformed from voluntary corporate social responsibility initiatives into structured regulatory and financial mechanisms.

Originally framed as reputational tools, ESG has evolved into:

- Investment risk assessment
- Regulatory compliance requirement
- Corporate governance benchmark
- Capital allocation filter

The transition reflects recognition that environmental and social risks translate into financial risks.

32.2 The Origins of ESG

The term ESG gained prominence through institutional investment discussions in the early 2000s, particularly under the United Nations Principles for Responsible Investment (PRI).

The PRI encouraged investors to integrate environmental, social and governance factors into investment decisions.

This marked a shift from philanthropy to fiduciary duty.

32.3 ESG as Risk Management

Climate volatility, supply chain disruption, litigation exposure, and regulatory tightening have reframed sustainability as material financial risk.

Environmental risk categories include:

- Carbon transition risk
- Physical climate risk
- Biodiversity loss
- Resource scarcity

Governance failures amplify environmental exposure.

CHAPTER 33

ESG DISCLOSURE AND GLOBAL STANDARDISATION

33.1 The Standardisation Challenge

Early ESG reporting suffered from fragmentation.

Different rating agencies used inconsistent methodologies, producing incomparable scores.

Standardisation became necessary.

33.2 International Sustainability Standards

The creation of the International Sustainability Standards Board (ISSB) marked a significant development.

ISSB standards aim to:

- Harmonise global disclosure frameworks
- Align sustainability reporting with financial reporting
- Enhance investor comparability

This regulatory shift transforms ESG into structured disclosure law.

33.3 European Regulatory Developments

The European Union introduced mandatory sustainability reporting obligations under its Corporate Sustainability Reporting Directive (CSRD).

This strengthens:

- Double materiality assessment
- Assurance requirements
- Digital reporting standards

The EU has become a global ESG regulatory leader.

CHAPTER 34

SUSTAINABLE FINANCE AND CAPITAL ALLOCATION

34.1 The Rise of Green Finance

Sustainable finance integrates ESG considerations into capital markets.

Financial instruments include:

- Green bonds
- Sustainability-linked loans
- Climate funds
- Transition bonds

These instruments channel capital toward environmentally beneficial projects.

34.2 Green Bonds

Green bonds finance projects such as:

- Renewable energy
- Waste infrastructure
- Public transportation
- Energy efficiency upgrades

Issuance has grown significantly over the past decade.

Investors demand transparency regarding use of proceeds.

34.3 Carbon Pricing and Market Signals

Carbon pricing mechanisms internalise emission costs.

Two major models:

- Carbon tax
- Emissions trading systems

Such mechanisms align with international climate commitments under the Paris Agreement.

Carbon markets influence investment flows and industrial strategy.

CHAPTER 35

CORPORATE GOVERNANCE AND BOARD RESPONSIBILITY

35.1 Directors' Duties and Sustainability

Corporate boards increasingly face expectations to integrate sustainability into strategic planning.

Climate litigation and shareholder activism reinforce accountability.

Failure to address material climate risk may expose directors to fiduciary challenges.

35.2 Executive Incentives

Linking executive compensation to ESG targets strengthens implementation.

Performance metrics may include:

- Emission reductions
- Waste reduction targets
- Renewable energy adoption
- Supply chain transparency

Incentive alignment drives behavioural change.

35.3 Audit and Assurance

Third-party assurance enhances credibility of sustainability disclosures.

Independent verification reduces greenwashing risk.

Governance structures must embed oversight at board level.

CHAPTER 36

ESG AND EMERGING MARKETS

36.1 Capital Flow and Competitiveness

Investors increasingly allocate capital toward jurisdictions demonstrating regulatory clarity and ESG credibility.

Emerging markets must balance:

- Development priorities
- Infrastructure needs
- Environmental responsibility

Sustainability frameworks enhance global investment attractiveness.

36.2 Malaysia's ESG Development

Malaysia has advanced sustainable finance initiatives through:

- Green sukuk issuance
- ESG reporting guidance
- Central bank climate risk integration

Sustainability positioning strengthens regional competitiveness.

36.3 ASEAN Regional Alignment

Harmonised ESG standards within ASEAN could:

- Reduce compliance complexity
- Increase cross-border investment
- Enhance regional capital markets

Regional cooperation strengthens resilience.

CHAPTER 37

GREENWASHING AND REGULATORY INTEGRITY

37.1 The Greenwashing Risk

As ESG demand increases, so does the risk of misrepresentation.

Greenwashing undermines:

- Investor confidence
- Regulatory credibility
- Market integrity

Clear disclosure standards are essential.

37.2 Regulatory Enforcement

Supervisory authorities must:

- Monitor ESG claims
- Impose penalties for misrepresentation
- Require transparent data

Strong enforcement maintains market trust.

37.3 Litigation Trends

Climate-related litigation is increasing globally.

Shareholders and civil society organisations are challenging corporate climate strategies.

Legal accountability is shaping corporate behaviour.

CHAPTER 38

INTEGRATION OF ESG AND CIRCULAR ECONOMY

38.1 ESG Metrics and Resource Efficiency

Circular economy indicators can be integrated into ESG reporting:

- Material intensity
- Recycling rate
- Waste diversion
- Product lifecycle metrics

This integration enhances reporting depth.

38.2 Scope 3 Emissions and Supply Chains

Scope 3 emissions include indirect emissions across supply chains.

Measurement challenges remain significant.

However, supply chain transparency is central to ESG credibility.

38.3 Technology and Data Governance

Digital monitoring systems improve ESG data accuracy.

AI and blockchain enhance traceability.

Technological integration strengthens accountability.

CHAPTER 39

CLIMATE FINANCE AND TRANSITION STRATEGY

39.1 Just Transition Principles

Climate transition must consider:

- Workforce displacement
- Community impact
- Social equity

Financial mechanisms should support inclusive transformation.

39.2 Transition Finance

Transition finance supports high-emitting industries shifting toward lower-carbon models.

This prevents abrupt economic disruption.

Strategic financing ensures gradual decarbonisation.

39.3 Global Financial Stability

Central banks increasingly integrate climate risk into macroprudential supervision.

Environmental risk is now recognised as systemic financial risk.

Sustainability is therefore linked to financial stability.

Concluding Reflection

ESG is no longer a peripheral reporting exercise.

It is:

- A regulatory requirement
- A capital market filter
- A governance reform tool
- A risk management framework

Corporate sustainability has become structurally embedded within global finance architecture.

Sustainability and finance are no longer separate domains they are interdependent.

PART VI

MALAYSIA IN THE GLOBAL SUSTAINABILITY LANDSCAPE

CHAPTER 40

MALAYSIA'S SUSTAINABILITY TRAJECTORY

40.1 Introduction: Development and Environmental Balancing

Malaysia's sustainability pathway reflects the broader challenge faced by emerging economies: balancing economic growth with environmental stewardship.

Since independence, Malaysia has prioritised:

- Industrialisation
- Export-led growth
- Infrastructure development
- Poverty reduction

These policies successfully improved income levels and living standards. However, rapid growth also intensified:

- Resource extraction
- Land-use change
- Urban waste generation
- Carbon emissions

The next phase of development requires structural integration of sustainability into national planning.

40.2 Institutional Framework

Malaysia's environmental governance operates through a combination of federal and state authority.

Key institutions include:

- Ministry of Natural Resources and Environmental Sustainability
- Department of Environment
- Securities Commission Malaysia
- Bank Negara Malaysia

Institutional coordination remains critical for policy coherence.

40.3 Legal Architecture

Malaysia's environmental regulation is anchored in the Environmental Quality Act 1974.

The Act provides mechanisms for:

- Pollution control
- Environmental impact assessment
- Licensing and enforcement

While foundational, evolving climate and circular economy challenges require modernisation.

CHAPTER 41

CLIMATE COMMITMENTS AND INTERNATIONAL ALIGNMENT

41.1 Global Commitments

Malaysia is a Party to the United Nations Framework Convention on Climate Change and the Paris Agreement.

Under the Paris Agreement, Malaysia submitted nationally determined contributions (NDCs) outlining emission reduction targets relative to GDP intensity.

International alignment shapes domestic policy direction.

41.2 National Energy Transition

Malaysia's energy mix remains partially dependent on fossil fuels.

However, renewable energy targets and solar expansion programmes are progressing.

Energy transition strategies must balance:

- Grid stability
- Industrial competitiveness
- Energy affordability
- Carbon reduction

Investment in clean energy infrastructure is central to climate mitigation.

41.3 Adaptation and Resilience

Climate risks affecting Malaysia include:

- Flooding
- Coastal erosion
- Heat stress
- Biodiversity loss

Adaptation planning must integrate into urban development, agriculture, and infrastructure design.

CHAPTER 42

CIRCULAR ECONOMY AND WASTE GOVERNANCE IN MALAYSIA

42.1 Waste Management Landscape

Urbanisation has increased municipal waste generation.

Challenges include:

- Landfill dependency
- Limited recycling infrastructure
- Public awareness gaps

Reform must integrate:

- Waste hierarchy principles
- Producer responsibility frameworks
- Data-driven monitoring

42.2 Prospects for Extended Producer Responsibility

EPR development in Malaysia remains at an emerging stage.

Successful implementation requires:

- Legislative amendment
- Industry consultation
- Compliance systems
- Enforcement capacity

EPR can stimulate domestic recycling markets and reduce environmental leakage.

42.3 Informal Sector Integration

Informal waste collectors contribute significantly to recycling rates.

Formal integration improves:

- Worker safety
- Data accuracy
- System efficiency

Inclusive transition strengthens governance outcomes.

CHAPTER 43

SUSTAINABLE FINANCE AND ESG IN MALAYSIA

43.1 Islamic Finance and Green Sukuk

Malaysia has positioned itself as a global leader in Islamic finance.

Green sukuk instruments combine Shariah-compliant finance with sustainability objectives.

These instruments finance:

- Renewable energy
- Sustainable infrastructure
- Environmental projects

Sustainable Islamic finance enhances Malaysia's global competitiveness.

43.2 Regulatory Guidance

Securities Commission Malaysia and Bank Negara Malaysia have introduced climate and ESG disclosure guidance.

Financial sector integration strengthens risk assessment and investor confidence.

43.3 Regional Capital Positioning

As ASEAN economies develop sustainability frameworks, Malaysia can position itself as:

- Regional green finance hub
- ESG reporting leader
- Carbon market participant

Strategic leadership enhances long-term economic resilience.

CHAPTER 44

BIODIVERSITY, FORESTRY AND NATURAL CAPITAL

44.1 Ecological Significance

Malaysia is one of the world's biodiversity-rich nations.

Its forests contribute to:

- Carbon sequestration
- Water regulation
- Species conservation

Balancing economic use and conservation remains a governance challenge.

44.2 Palm Oil and Global Scrutiny

Palm oil production has drawn international attention regarding deforestation concerns.

Sustainable certification schemes aim to improve environmental performance.

Trade relationships increasingly incorporate sustainability criteria.

44.3 **Nature-Based Solutions**

Reforestation and mangrove restoration provide:

- Carbon storage
- Coastal protection
- Biodiversity benefits

Nature-based solutions integrate climate mitigation with ecological resilience.

CHAPTER 45

INDUSTRIAL POLICY AND GREEN COMPETITIVENESS

45.1 Export Markets and Sustainability Standards

Major trading partners increasingly require sustainability compliance.

Environmental standards affect:

- Supply chain access
- Export competitiveness
- Investment flows

Domestic reform strengthens international positioning.

45.2 Technology and Innovation

Malaysia's innovation ecosystem can support:

- Renewable energy manufacturing
- Recycling technologies
- ESG data platforms

Technology adoption enhances productivity and environmental performance.

45.3 Workforce Transition

Green transition requires:

- Skills development
- Education reform
- Workforce retraining

Human capital investment underpins long-term transformation.

CHAPTER 46

GOVERNANCE REFORM AND INSTITUTIONAL CAPACITY

46.1 Inter-Agency Coordination

Fragmented implementation reduces policy effectiveness.

Coordinated national strategy enhances impact.

Whole-of-government approaches are necessary.

46.2 Data and Transparency

Reliable environmental data supports:

- Investor confidence
- Policy evaluation
- International credibility

Digital reporting systems improve oversight.

46.3 Public Participation

Citizen engagement strengthens accountability.

Transparency fosters trust in sustainability governance.

CHAPTER 47

MALAYSIA'S ROLE IN ASEAN AND GLOBAL FORUMS

47.1 ASEAN Sustainability Cooperation

Regional collaboration can harmonise:

- ESG standards
- Waste regulation
- Renewable energy trade

Collective progress reduces regulatory fragmentation.

47.2 Global Leadership Opportunities

Malaysia can leverage its:

- Islamic finance expertise
- Biodiversity assets
- Regional diplomatic position

Strategic engagement enhances influence in global sustainability discussions.

Concluding Reflection

Malaysia stands at a strategic inflection point.

Its development success provides capacity for sustainability reform.

Global trade dynamics, climate risk, and capital flows increasingly reward environmental credibility.

Malaysia's long-term competitiveness depends on:

- Regulatory clarity
- Sustainable finance integration
- Circular economy adoption
- Climate resilience planning
- Institutional coordination

Sustainability is no longer peripheral to national development. It is central to economic strategy.

PART VII

SUSTAINABLE LIFESTYLES AND BEHAVIOURAL CHANGE

CHAPTER 48

WHY SYSTEMS CHANGE REQUIRES BEHAVIOUR CHANGE

48.1 Beyond Policy and Corporate Reform

Public policy and corporate governance are critical pillars of sustainability reform. However, systemic transformation cannot occur without behavioural change at the individual and community level.

Consumption patterns influence:

- Waste generation
- Carbon emissions
- Energy demand
- Resource extraction

Sustainability is therefore both structural and behavioural.

48.2 The Behaviour–Policy Feedback Loop

Policy shapes behaviour.

Behaviour influences political will.

For example:

- Plastic bans alter consumer purchasing patterns
- Carbon pricing influences transport choices
- Recycling mandates shift household waste sorting

Behavioural adoption strengthens policy legitimacy.

48.3 The Psychology of Environmental Action

Behavioural economics demonstrates that individuals do not always act rationally in environmental contexts.

Barriers include:

- Convenience bias
- Cost perception
- Social norms
- Information asymmetry

Understanding these psychological dimensions enables effective intervention design.

CHAPTER 49

CONSUMPTION, IDENTITY AND MODERN LIFESTYLES

49.1 Consumer Culture and Materialism

Modern economic systems have historically equated consumption with prosperity.

Advertising, digital platforms, and social media amplify aspirational consumption.

However, excessive consumption contributes to:

- Resource depletion
- Carbon emissions
- Waste accumulation

Reframing prosperity is central to sustainability.

49.2 Minimalism and Conscious Consumption

Emerging lifestyle movements promote:

- Repair over replacement
- Sharing economies
- Slow fashion
- Low-waste living

Such practices align with circular economy principles.

49.3 Digital Influence and Social Norms

Digital platforms shape behavioural norms rapidly.

Online communities can accelerate sustainable practices through:

- Peer influence
- Transparency
- Collective accountability

Behavioural diffusion is increasingly network-driven.

CHAPTER 50

ENERGY USE AND HOUSEHOLD CARBON FOOTPRINT

50.1 Residential Energy Behaviour

Household energy consumption represents a significant portion of national emissions.

Behavioural interventions include:

- Energy-efficient appliances
- Smart meters
- Demand-side management
- Rooftop solar adoption

Energy literacy enhances adoption.

50.2 Transport Choices

Private vehicle dependency increases emissions.

Behavioural shifts toward:

- Public transport
- Carpooling
- Electric vehicles
- Active mobility (walking, cycling)

Reduce carbon intensity.

50.3 Food Systems and Diet

Dietary patterns affect land use and emissions.

Reducing food waste and increasing plant-based consumption lowers environmental impact.

Food system awareness influences consumer demand and supply chains.

CHAPTER 51

WASTE, RECYCLING AND HOUSEHOLD RESPONSIBILITY

51.1 Waste Sorting Behaviour

Recycling systems fail without public participation.

Clear labelling, convenient infrastructure, and consistent enforcement improve compliance.

Behavioural nudges can increase recycling rates.

51.2 Single-Use Plastics

Individual reduction of single-use plastics complements regulatory bans.

Reusable alternatives reduce waste leakage into marine ecosystems.

51.3 Composting and Organic Waste

Organic waste diversion reduces landfill methane emissions.

Community composting programmes enhance local participation.

CHAPTER 52

EDUCATION AND INTERGENERATIONAL CHANGE

52.1 Environmental Education

Integrating sustainability into school curricula cultivates long-term behavioural transformation.

Youth engagement influences household behaviour.

52.2 Universities and Research Culture

Higher education institutions serve as:

- Knowledge hubs
- Policy advisors
- Innovation incubators

Campus sustainability practices model institutional responsibility.

52.3 Intergenerational Equity

Sustainability ethics are grounded in responsibility toward future generations.

This principle underpins global climate governance frameworks such as the Paris Agreement.

CHAPTER 53

COMMUNITY ACTION AND LOCAL GOVERNANCE

53.1 Urban Sustainability Initiatives

Cities are central to sustainability transformation.

Local initiatives include:

- Zero-waste neighbourhoods
- Urban farming
- Renewable energy cooperatives

Local action reinforces national strategy.

53.2 Civil Society and Advocacy

Non-governmental organisations influence policy reform and corporate accountability.

Community mobilisation increases democratic participation.

53.3 Faith, Culture and Sustainability

Cultural and religious values shape environmental ethics.

In Malaysia's plural society, sustainability messaging can align with shared moral frameworks.

Values-based engagement enhances behavioural adoption.

CHAPTER 54

DIGITAL TECHNOLOGY AND BEHAVIOURAL NUDGING

54.1 Smart Data and Personalised Feedback

Smart devices provide real-time environmental impact data.

Personalised feedback encourages:

- Reduced electricity consumption
- Lower water usage
- Sustainable purchasing decisions

Data transparency enhances accountability.

54.2 Behavioural Economics and Policy Design

Governments increasingly apply behavioural insights:

- Default green energy options
- Plastic bag charges
- Incentive-based recycling systems

Small design changes yield significant impact.

54.3 Ethical Considerations

Behavioural nudging must respect:

- Autonomy
- Privacy
- Transparency

Ethical governance safeguards public trust.

CHAPTER 55

BARRIERS TO BEHAVIOURAL CHANGE

55.1 Structural Constraints

Low-income households may face affordability barriers.

Infrastructure limitations constrain sustainable choices.

Policy must ensure equitable access.

55.2 Green Fatigue and Misinformation

Public fatigue and misinformation undermine sustained engagement.

Consistent communication and credible data reduce scepticism.

55.3 Trust in Institutions

Behavioural adoption depends on institutional credibility.

Transparency and enforcement strengthen public cooperation.

CHAPTER 56

FROM INDIVIDUAL ACTION TO COLLECTIVE TRANSFORMATION

56.1 The Power of Collective Behaviour

Individual behaviour aggregates into systemic influence.

Consumer demand drives corporate reform.

Electoral choices shape policy direction.

56.2 Linking Lifestyle to ESG and Corporate Reform

Sustainable lifestyles influence:

- Investor expectations
- Brand reputation
- Supply chain practices

Consumer activism intersects with corporate governance.

56.3 Toward a Culture of Sustainability

Long-term transformation requires cultural integration of sustainability values into daily life.

Sustainability must become normative rather than exceptional.

Concluding Reflection

Behavioural change is neither trivial nor secondary.

It is foundational.

While governments regulate and corporations invest, citizens:

- Consume
- Vote
- Influence markets
- Shape social norms

Sustainable development ultimately depends on cultural transformation as much as institutional reform.

A sustainable future requires alignment between:

- Policy
- Corporate governance
- Financial systems
- Community values
- Individual choices

Only when these dimensions converge does transformation become durable.

PART VIII

THE FUTURE – SYSTEMS TRANSFORMATION

CHAPTER 57

FROM INCREMENTAL REFORM TO SYSTEMIC TRANSFORMATION

57.1 The Limits of Incrementalism

Over the past three decades, sustainability governance has largely progressed through incremental reform:

- Emission reduction targets
- Voluntary ESG reporting
- Recycling campaigns
- Corporate pledges

While valuable, incremental measures have not reversed global environmental degradation at sufficient speed.

Climate volatility, biodiversity collapse, and resource scarcity indicate structural imbalances.

Systemic challenges require systemic responses.

57.2 What Is Systems Transformation?

Systems transformation refers to coordinated change across:

- Economic structures
- Regulatory frameworks
- Financial systems
- Technological infrastructure
- Cultural norms

It recognises interdependence rather than isolated sector reform.

57.3 The Complexity of Interconnected Risks

Environmental crises intersect with:

- Economic inequality
- Food security
- Energy stability
- Migration patterns

Integrated policy architecture is therefore essential.

CHAPTER 58

RETHINKING ECONOMIC GROWTH

58.1 Growth Versus Sustainability

Traditional economic models prioritise GDP expansion.

However, GDP growth does not account for:

- Environmental degradation
- Natural capital depletion
- Social inequality

Alternative metrics are increasingly debated.

58.2 Natural Capital Accounting

Natural capital accounting integrates ecological value into national financial systems.

Forests, water resources, and biodiversity become measurable assets.

This enables:

- Informed policy decisions
- Transparent trade-offs
- Long-term fiscal planning

58.3 Circular and Regenerative Models

Regenerative economic frameworks extend beyond reducing harm.

They aim to:

- Restore ecosystems
- Enhance biodiversity
- Strengthen resilience

Circular economy principles provide a foundation for this transformation.

CHAPTER 59

CLIMATE GOVERNANCE IN A FRAGMENTED WORLD

59.1 Multilateralism Under Pressure

Global climate governance operates through multilateral frameworks such as the Paris Agreement.

However, geopolitical tensions and uneven ambition create coordination challenges.

National interests often conflict with collective climate objectives.

59.2 Carbon Border Adjustments and Trade

Emerging carbon border measures reflect efforts to prevent carbon leakage.

Such instruments reshape global trade dynamics.

Export-oriented economies must adapt to evolving regulatory landscapes.

59.3 Financing the Transition

Global climate finance gaps remain substantial.

Bridging these gaps requires:

- Public-private partnerships
- Multilateral development banks
- Sovereign green bonds
- Private capital mobilisation

Financial innovation is central to transformation.

CHAPTER 60

TECHNOLOGY, INNOVATION AND DIGITAL ACCELERATION

60.1 Clean Energy Innovation

Advances in:

- Solar photovoltaics
- Battery storage
- Green hydrogen
- Smart grids

are accelerating decarbonisation potential.

Technology reduces cost barriers over time.

60.2 Artificial Intelligence and Sustainability

AI enhances:

- Energy optimisation
- Supply chain transparency
- Climate modelling
- ESG data verification

However, digital expansion also carries energy and governance implications.

60.3 Ethical Technology Governance

Emerging technologies require oversight to ensure:

- Data privacy
- Equity
- Environmental net benefit

Governance must evolve alongside innovation.

CHAPTER 61

SOCIAL JUSTICE AND JUST TRANSITION

61.1 The Equity Dimension

Environmental reform must address social equity.

Transition policies must protect:

- Workers in carbon-intensive industries
- Low-income households
- Vulnerable communities

Sustainability without justice risks social instability.

61.2 Intergenerational Responsibility

Future generations bear consequences of present decisions.

This ethical foundation shapes international climate commitments and constitutional environmental rights in some jurisdictions.

61.3 Inclusive Policymaking

Participatory governance strengthens legitimacy.

Community consultation improves implementation success.

Equitable transition builds long-term resilience.

CHAPTER 62

GOVERNANCE REFORM FOR THE 21ST CENTURY

62.1 Whole-of-Government Approaches

Sustainability integration requires cross-ministerial coordination.

Environmental objectives must align with:

- Industrial policy
- Trade strategy
- Education reform
- Fiscal planning

Policy silos weaken outcomes.

62.2 Data-Driven Decision-Making

Reliable environmental metrics enable:

- Evidence-based policy
- Transparent monitoring
- Adaptive regulation

Digital governance infrastructure strengthens accountability.

62.3 Corporate–State Collaboration

Private sector engagement is essential.

Public policy sets direction.

Corporate innovation scales implementation.

Collaborative governance bridges capacity gaps.

CHAPTER 63

CULTURAL TRANSFORMATION AND NARRATIVE CHANGE

63.1 Shifting Public Imagination

Societal narratives shape policy acceptance.

Framing sustainability as opportunity rather than sacrifice enhances adoption.

63.2 Media, Education and Leadership

Educational institutions and media platforms influence long-term mindset change.

Leadership credibility determines reform durability.

63.3 The Role of Values

Sustainability ultimately rests on normative commitments:

- Stewardship
- Responsibility
- Equity
- Long-term thinking

Cultural alignment strengthens systemic reform.

CHAPTER 64

MALAYSIA'S STRATEGIC FUTURE POSITIONING

64.1 Regional Leadership Potential

Malaysia can integrate:

- Green finance leadership
- Circular economy development
- Renewable energy expansion
- Biodiversity protection

Strategic positioning enhances resilience.

64.2 Economic Competitiveness in a Low-Carbon Era

Future trade competitiveness will depend on:

- Carbon intensity
- ESG transparency
- Regulatory clarity

Proactive reform reduces transition risk.

64.3 A National Sustainability Blueprint

Long-term transformation may require:

- Updated legislative frameworks
- Integrated sustainability targets
- Public accountability mechanisms

Strategic planning ensures continuity beyond political cycles.

Concluding Chapter

Toward a Regenerative Future

Systems transformation is not a singular policy reform.

It is an alignment of:

- Economic incentives
- Legal structures
- Financial flows
- Technological innovation
- Cultural values

The sustainability challenge is not merely environmental.

It is civilisational.

The future will be shaped by how effectively governments, corporations, communities, and individuals coordinate their actions within planetary boundaries.

For Malaysia and the wider global community, the opportunity is historic:

To transition from extractive growth

To regenerative prosperity

To move from fragmented policy

To integrated systems governance

To build not merely a sustainable economy

But a resilient and just society

SPECIAL THEMATIC CHAPTER

University of Cambridge

Dr. Jayaprakash Murulitharan

Author of the PhD thesis ***"Assessing $PM_{2.5}$ Pollution and the Role of Transboundary Emissions Across Greater Kuala Lumpur, Malaysia (2018–2023)"****, Yusuf Hamied Department of Chemistry, University of Cambridge (2025).*

Atmospheric Science and the Dynamics of Air Quality in Southeast Asia

Atmospheric science examines the physical and chemical processes that govern the Earth's atmosphere and their interactions with natural and human systems. The atmosphere is a complex and dynamic system composed primarily of nitrogen (78%), oxygen (21%), argon, and trace gases, continuously interacting with oceans, vegetation, and biological systems that regulate the planet's climatic balance. Understanding these interactions is fundamental to interpreting weather patterns, air quality, and long-term climate dynamics.

My research and expertise is assessing the burden of air pollution within urban cities in Malaysia, particularly during transboundary haze events.

One of the most critical concerns within atmospheric science today is air pollution, particularly the presence of fine particulate matter known as $PM_{2.5}$. These microscopic particles, measuring less than 2.5 micrometres in diameter, originate from both natural processes and anthropogenic activities such as industrial emissions, transportation, biomass burning, and residential fuel combustion. Due to their extremely small size, $PM_{2.5}$ particles can penetrate deep into the human respiratory system, contributing to severe health impacts, including respiratory and cardiovascular diseases. Atmospheric pollution, therefore, represents not only an environmental issue but also a major global public health challenge.

In Southeast Asia, the complexity of atmospheric processes is further intensified by rapid urbanisation, industrial growth, and regional climatic conditions. Major metropolitan regions, such as Greater Kuala Lumpur, experience fluctuating air quality due to interactions between local emission sources and long-range atmospheric transport. Under specific meteorological conditions, pollutants generated hundreds of kilometres away can be transported across national boundaries, contributing to the regional phenomenon known as transboundary haze.

Research on atmospheric dispersion modelling and emission inventories has shown that large-scale biomass burning events in parts of Sumatera significantly influence $PM_{2.5}$ concentrations across Malaysia. Atmospheric circulation patterns, particularly seasonal monsoon winds, transport smoke and aerosols from fire-affected regions into urban centres. Studies using numerical atmospheric models demonstrate that during major haze episodes, provinces such as Riau and Jambi can contribute substantially to particulate pollution observed in Greater Kuala Lumpur.

These findings highlight the importance of atmospheric science in informing environmental governance and regional policy cooperation. Air pollution does not recognise political borders, and therefore, addressing transboundary atmospheric pollution requires collaborative scientific monitoring, data sharing, and coordinated policy responses among neighbouring countries. Advances in satellite observation, atmospheric modelling, and emission inventory analysis now allow scientists to better understand pollutant transport pathways and quantify the sources contributing to regional air quality deterioration.

Ultimately, atmospheric science provides the evidence base needed to design effective environmental policies, improve public health protection, and guide sustainable urban development. As Southeast Asia continues to grow economically and demographically, strengthening atmospheric research capacity will be essential for managing air quality, mitigating climate impacts, and ensuring a resilient and sustainable future.

EXECUTIVE CONCLUSION

Toward an Integrated Sustainability Architecture

1. The Structural Imperative

This book has demonstrated that sustainability is no longer a peripheral environmental concern. It is a structural economic, legal, financial and governance imperative.

Across Parts I–VIII, we have examined:

- Climate governance under the Paris Agreement
- Circular economy frameworks and waste reform
- Extended Producer Responsibility (EPR) policy instruments
- ESG standardisation through the International Sustainability Standards Board
- Sustainable finance mechanisms
- Malaysia's regional positioning
- Behavioural transformation
- Systems-level economic restructuring

The conclusion is clear:

Environmental risk has become financial risk.

Financial risk has become systemic risk.

Systemic risk demands coordinated governance.

Incremental reform, while necessary, is insufficient.

The future requires integrated sustainability architecture.

2. The Convergence of Five Pillars

Effective transformation depends on the convergence of five structural pillars:

Pillar 1: Regulatory Modernisation

Environmental legislation must evolve beyond pollution control toward:

- Carbon accountability
- Circular resource governance
- Mandatory sustainability disclosure
- Digital environmental reporting

Clear enforcement enhances investor and public confidence.

Pillar 2: Financial Realignment

Capital markets must internalise environmental risk through:

- ESG disclosure mandates
- Climate stress testing
- Green bond frameworks
- Carbon pricing instruments

Sustainable finance directs capital toward long-term resilience.

Pillar 3: Industrial and Technological Transition

Economic competitiveness in a low-carbon era depends on:

- Renewable energy expansion
- Clean technology innovation
- Circular manufacturing systems
- Sustainable infrastructure investment

Industrial policy must align with decarbonisation.

Pillar 4: Institutional Coordination

Fragmented governance weakens sustainability reform.

Whole-of-government integration is required across:

- Trade
- Finance
- Environment
- Energy
- Education

Policy coherence reduces regulatory contradiction.

Pillar 5: Cultural and Behavioural Alignment

Sustainability is not solely institutional.

It is societal.

Consumer demand, civic engagement, and ethical values shape market direction and political will.

Behavioural change reinforces systemic reform.

POLICY ROADMAP SUMMARY

A Strategic 10–20 Year Transition Framework

The following roadmap provides structured guidance for phased transformation.

Phase I (0–5 Years): Foundation and Regulatory Alignment

1. **Legislative Review and Modernisation**
    - Update environmental statutes to incorporate climate and circular economy provisions
    - Introduce formal EPR legislation
    - Mandate sustainability disclosure aligned with international standards
2. **National Carbon Strategy**
    - Develop carbon pricing roadmap
    - Establish transparent emission measurement infrastructure
    - Align NDC commitments under the United Nations Framework Convention on Climate Change
3. **ESG Regulatory Integration**
    - Adopt ISSB-aligned disclosure standards
    - Strengthen corporate governance codes
    - Enhance anti-greenwashing enforcement
4. **Data Infrastructure Investment**
    - Develop national environmental data platform
    - Digitise waste tracking systems
    - Improve climate risk modelling capacity

Phase II (5–10 Years): Market Transformation and Scale

1. **Renewable Energy Expansion**
    - Accelerate grid modernisation
    - Increase solar and storage deployment
    - Support clean hydrogen research
2. **Circular Economy Implementation**
    - Operationalise EPR schemes across packaging and electronics
    - Incentivise recycled material markets
    - Integrate informal sector participants
3. **Sustainable Finance Leadership**
    - Expand green sukuk and bond issuance
    - Implement climate stress testing in banking sector
    - Develop carbon trading mechanisms
4. **Workforce and Education Reform**
    - Introduce green skills training programmes
    - Embed sustainability in national curricula
    - Support workforce transition pathways

Phase III (10–20 Years): Systems Integration and Regenerative Development

1. **Natural Capital Accounting**
    - Integrate ecosystem valuation into national budgeting
    - Develop biodiversity performance indicators
2. **Full Industrial Decarbonisation Pathways**
    - Support heavy industry transition financing
    - Encourage circular production design

3. **Regional and Global Leadership**
    - Position Malaysia as ASEAN sustainability hub
    - Lead in Islamic sustainable finance innovation
    - Contribute actively to multilateral climate negotiations
4. **Cultural Institutionalisation**
    - Normalize sustainability metrics in corporate reporting
    - Institutionalise ESG-linked executive remuneration
    - Embed environmental ethics within public administration

Strategic Outcomes

If implemented coherently, this roadmap can deliver:

- Enhanced export competitiveness
- Increased foreign investment
- Reduced climate vulnerability
- Strengthened fiscal resilience
- Improved public health
- Long-term ecological stability

Sustainability reform is not economic sacrifice.

It is economic modernisation.

Final Reflection

The transition ahead is complex but unavoidable.

The global economy is undergoing structural recalibration.

Capital markets are repricing environmental risk.

Trade systems are incorporating carbon accountability.

Citizens are demanding corporate transparency.

Malaysia and the broader global community faces a strategic choice:

To react defensively to external regulatory pressure or to lead proactively in shaping sustainable growth

The opportunity is not merely environmental compliance.

It is generational transformation.

A sustainable future will not emerge through isolated reforms.

It will emerge through coordinated systems governance where law, finance, industry, culture, and ethics align within planetary boundaries.

The task is ambitious. But it is achievable. And it is necessary.

SYSTEMS TRANSFORMATION FOR A SUSTAINABLE FUTURE

A National Policy Roadmap for Integrated Sustainability Governance

Author: Dr. Sri Umeswaran Shekar

Policy White Paper

Executive Summary

This policy white paper outlines a structured 10 to 20 year roadmap for national sustainability transformation. It recognises that environmental risk has evolved into financial and systemic risk, requiring coordinated reform across regulatory, financial, industrial, and social domains.

The framework integrates climate governance, circular economy reform, ESG disclosure standards, sustainable finance mobilisation, and behavioural alignment into a unified national strategy.

Five Pillars of Systems Transformation

1. Regulatory Modernisation: Updating environmental laws to incorporate carbon accountability, circular economy mechanisms, and mandatory sustainability disclosure.
2. Financial Realignment: Embedding ESG disclosure, climate stress testing, green bonds, and carbon pricing into capital allocation systems.
3. Industrial & Technological Transition: Expanding renewable energy, clean technologies, circular production systems, and sustainable infrastructure.

4. Institutional Coordination: Implementing whole-of-government policy integration across finance, trade, energy, education, and environment.
5. Cultural & Behavioural Alignment: Encouraging sustainable consumption, education reform, and long-term ethical responsibility.

Strategic Policy Roadmap (10–20 Years)

Phase I (0–5 Years): Foundation & Regulatory Alignment

- Modernise environmental legislation.
- Establish national carbon measurement infrastructure.
- Align ESG disclosure with international standards.
- Develop national environmental data systems.

Phase II (5–10 Years): Market Transformation & Scaling

- Accelerate renewable energy deployment.
- Operationalise Extended Producer Responsibility schemes.
- Expand green and sustainable finance instruments.
- Introduce national green workforce training programmes.

Phase III (10–20 Years): Systems Integration & Regeneration

- Integrate natural capital accounting into fiscal planning.
- Complete industrial decarbonisation pathways.
- Position Malaysia as a regional sustainability and green finance hub.
- Institutionalise ESG-linked governance practices.

Strategic Outcomes

If implemented coherently, this roadmap can deliver enhanced export competitiveness, greater foreign investment, reduced climate vulnerability, improved public health, fiscal resilience, and long-term ecological stability.

Sustainability reform is not economic sacrifice; it is structural economic modernisation. Proactive transformation positions the nation competitively within an evolving global low-carbon economy.

GLOSSARY

Adaptation	Policy and practical measures aimed at adjusting to actual or expected climate impacts to reduce harm or exploit beneficial opportunities.
Biodiversity	The variety of living organisms within ecosystems, species, and genetic variation.
Carbon Border Adjustment Mechanism (CBAM)	A trade policy instrument that applies carbon costs to imported goods to prevent carbon leakage.
Carbon Pricing	An economic instrument that assigns a cost to greenhouse gas emissions through taxes or trading systems.
Circular Economy	An economic model focused on resource efficiency, waste reduction, reuse, recycling, and regenerative design.
Climate Mitigation	Actions taken to reduce or prevent greenhouse gas emissions.
Double Materiality	A reporting principle requiring companies to disclose both how sustainability issues affect them financially and how their activities impact the environment and society.
Environmental, Social and Governance (ESG)	A framework used to assess corporate sustainability performance across environmental, social responsibility, and governance dimensions.
Extended Producer Responsibility (EPR)	A policy approach that makes producers responsible for the post-consumer phase of their products.
Green Finance	Financial investments directed toward sustainable development projects and initiatives.

Greenwashing	Misleading claims about environmental performance to create a false impression of sustainability.
Natural Capital	The world's stocks of natural resources, including forests, water, soil, and biodiversity, that provide ecosystem services.
Nationally Determined Contributions (NDCs)	National climate commitments submitted under the Paris Agreement.
Scope 1, 2 and 3 Emissions	Classification of greenhouse gas emissions based on direct and indirect sources within value chains.
Sustainable Development	Development that meets present needs without compromising the ability of future generations to meet their own needs.
Sustainable Finance	Financial services integrating ESG considerations into investment and lending decisions.
Waste Hierarchy	A prioritisation framework ranking waste management options: prevention, reduction, reuse, recycling, recovery, and disposal.

REFERENCES / BIBLIOGRAPHY

International Treaties and Instruments

Paris Agreement (adopted 12 December 2015, entered into force 4 November 2016)

United Nations Framework Convention on Climate Change (adopted 9 May 1992, entered into force 21 March 1994) 1771 UNTS 107

Convention on Biological Diversity (adopted 5 June 1992, entered into force 29 December 1993)

Basel Convention on the Control of Transboundary Movements of Hazardous Wastes and Their Disposal (1989)

International Materials

United Nations, *Transforming Our World: The 2030 Agenda for Sustainable Development* (UN 2015)

International Sustainability Standards Board, *IFRS S1 General Requirements for Disclosure of Sustainability-related Financial Information* (IFRS Foundation 2023)

International Sustainability Standards Board, *IFRS S2 Climate-related Disclosures* (IFRS Foundation 2023)

Organisation for Economic Co-operation and Development, *Extended Producer Responsibility: Updated Guidance for Efficient Waste Management* (OECD 2016)

World Bank, *State and Trends of Carbon Pricing 2023* (World Bank 2023)

European Commission, 'Corporate Sustainability Reporting Directive' (2022)

Legislation

Environmental Quality Act 1974 (Malaysia)

Corporate Sustainability Reporting Directive (Directive (EU) 2022/2464)

Books

Sachs JD, *The Age of Sustainable Development* (Columbia University Press 2015)

Stern N, *The Economics of Climate Change: The Stern Review* (Cambridge University Press 2007)

Raworth K, *Doughnut Economics* (Chelsea Green Publishing 2017)

Raworth K, *Doughnut Economics: Seven Ways to Think Like a 21st-Century Economist* (Chelsea Green Publishing 2017)

Geissdoerfer M and others, *The Circular Economy: A New Sustainability Paradigm?* (Routledge 2020).

Porter ME and van der Linde C, 'Green and Competitive' (1995) 33 Harvard Business Review

Elkington J, *Cannibals with Forks: The Triple Bottom Line of 21st Century Business* (Capstone 1997)

Ostrom E, *Governing the Commons* (Cambridge University Press 1990)

Journal Articles

Porter ME and Kramer MR, 'Creating Shared Value' (2011) 89(1/2) *Harvard Business Review* 62

Rockström J et al, 'Planetary Boundaries' (2009) 461 Nature 472

Carney M, 'Breaking the Tragedy of the Horizon Climate Change and Financial Stability' (2015) Speech at Lloyd's of London

Falkner R, 'The Paris Agreement and the New Logic of International Climate Politics' (2016) 92 International Affairs 1107

Policy & Institutional Reports

Bank Negara Malaysia, *Climate Change and Principle-based Taxonomy* (BNM 2021)

Securities Commission Malaysia, *Malaysian Code on Corporate Governance* (SC 2021)

United Nations Environment Programme, *Emissions Gap Report 2023* (UNEP 2023)

Intergovernmental Panel on Climate Change, *Sixth Assessment Report* (2021–2023)

World Bank, *State and Trends of Carbon Pricing* (latest edition)

International Energy Agency, *World Energy Outlook* (latest edition)

ABOUT THE AUTHOR

Dr. Sri Umeswaran Shekar is an internationally recognised expert in Circular Economy, Sustainability Governance, and Waste Management. He holds a PhD in Environmental Science Management with a specialisation in Circular Economy, a Diploma in Integrative Journalism, and is a certified Marine Ecologist and Naturalist awarded by the International Association of Nitrox & Technical Divers (IANTD). He is currently pursuing a Bachelor of Laws (LLB) and Master of Laws (LLM) to strengthen environmental policy integration.

He serves in national leadership roles and advises on waste management, circular economy and sustainability frameworks. As a passionate advocate, he actively shares his knowledge through publications, conferences, and media engagements to advance global environmental sustainability.

He is the author of 'Love the Environment' (Sutrusoolalai Nesipom), the first bilingual book on environmental awareness published in Tamil and English in Malaysia and continues to contribute to national and international policy dialogues, academic lectures, and sustainability initiatives aimed at advancing global environmental goals.

Preferred method of contact:

Email: sriumeswaran@gmail.com

LinkedIn: https://www.linkedin.com/in/s-sriumeswara/

www.ingramcontent.com/pod-product-compliance
Lightning Source LLC
LaVergne TN
LVHW090309210926
848480LV00001B/186
* 9 7 9 8 9 0 3 4 2 6 8 0 5 *